FRENCH EDUCATIONAL THEORISTS

BY

KEVORK A. SARAFIAN, Ph.D.

Head of Department of Education, LaVerne College. Lecturer in Education, Claremont Colleges. Lecturer in Education, Summer Sessions, University of Southern California.

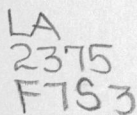

PUBLISHED BY C. C. CRAWFORD

UNIVERSITY OF SOUTHERN CALIFORNIA   LOS ANGELES, CALIFORNIA

COPYRIGHT 1933
BY KEVORK A. SARAFIAN
ALL RIGHTS RESERVED

PRINTED IN U. S. A.
PRESS OF THE LA VERNE LEADER
LAVERNE, CALIF.
1933

Dedicated
with affection and respect
to the
memory of my
Mother and Father

CONTENTS

CHAPTER I

François Rabelais
Rabelais' Personality 11
Biography of Rabelais 17
Gargantua and Pantagruel 19
Educational Ideas of Rabelais Based on Quotations from Gargantua and Pantagruel 20
Education Through Real Things 28
Physical Education 28
School Excursions 29
Pleasant Methods 29
Religious and Moral Education 30
Nature Good, Hence Freedom 31
Encyclopedic Knowledge 32
Curriculum 32
Educational Influences of Rabelais 34
Bossuet and Fénelon Compared 35

CHAPTER II

Michel De Montaigne
Montaigne's Personality 38
Some Important Essays 39
Biography of Montaigne 41
Educational Ideas of Montaigne 44
Education of the Whole Man 44
Education is not a Pouring-in Process 45
Training of the Judgment and Understanding 47
Memory Work Condemned 48
Learning by Doing 49
Physical Exercise 50
The Place of Interest and Curiosity 51
Harsh Discipline Condemned 51
Moral Education 53
History and Languages 54
The Importance of Travel... 56

CONTENTS

World-Mindedness as an Aim 57
Montaigne's Influence 58

CHAPTER III

François Salagnac de La Mothe Fénelon

The Personality of Fénelon 61
Biography of Fénelon 63
Fénelon, "Quiétisme," and The Jansenists 64
Jacqueline Pascal and her "Réglements pour les Enfants de Port Royal" 66
Madame de Maintenon 68
De l'Education des Filles 69
Educational Ideals of Fénelon—the Need of Education for Women 72
Developing Judgment and Personality 73
Learning as Pleasurable Experience 74
Use of Right Motivation 75
Emphasis on Physical Education 76
Acute Observations of Human Nature.................... 76
Follow Nature 78
A Fine Method of Moral Education 78
Use of Stories in Character Formation—Telemachus 79
Object Lessons and Experiencing 81
Observations of Girls' Defects 82
The Curriculum 84
Fénelon's Success as a Tutor 85

CHAPTER IV

Jean-Jacques Rousseau

Personality of Rousseau 88
Divergent Views on Rousseau 90
Important Considerations in Judging Rousseau 92
The Three Fundamental Errors in Emile 93
The Historical Setting 93
The Child a Miniature Adult 95
Child's Nature and the Church 95
Rousseau's Own Reaction 96

CONTENTS

The Stronger the Persecution the Greater the Influence 98
Biography of Rousseau 100
Emile and The New Heloisa 105
Rousseau's Educational Ideas— Rousseau, the Emancipator of Childhood 107
Education as a Process of Living and not Merely Preparation 109
The Nature of the Child the Starting Point for Education 110
Memoriter Type of Education Condemned 114
Education by Direct Experiencing 115
The Importance of Physical Activities 116
Training of the Senses and the Objective Teaching 117
Methods in the Teaching of Specific Subjects 118
Industrial Education 121
Moral Training 122
Democratic Conceptions of Education 124

Bibliography 127-134

PREFACE

The works of the French educational thinkers are not very well known in the United States. A dirth and scantiness of first-hand information regarding the Gallic educationalists is conspicuous in our educational literature and it seems as though American educational historians, with few exceptions, accord little recognition to the contributions of these French theorists of education. It may be that the extreme conservativeness of the official French educational system has beclouded the vision and deterred the attention of our writers and teachers in the field of educational history from the eminently creative and progressive thoughts of the French educational philosophers. Yet in the evolution of our modern educational thought and practice these men have rendered very important contributions. On the one hand the work of Jean Jacques Rousseau is misapprehended and misinterpreted[1] by many of our American students in the field of the history of education; on the other hand the work of Fén-

---

[1] The writer, after twenty long years, still remembers the statement of his very beloved and able teacher in the History of Education in an excellent school in Massachusetts, concerning Jean-Jacques Rousseau, whom he characterized as an insane man and his work as unworthy of consideration in a class devoted to the discussion of the evolution of educational thought and practice.

elon is almost unknown to the rank and file of our educational workers.

This work is a modest attempt to bring into closer and fresher contact our American educators with the original sources and works of a few of the French theorists in education of international importance. The author has endeavored through copious citations from the writings of these men to offer an opportunity to the readers for a firsthand acquaintance with them. Most of the translations are done by the author himself into modern and current English of today. Trusting that his efforts will not prove entirely fruitless, he takes this opportunity to express his indebtedness to all masters in education, ancient and modern, foreign and American, whose works have inspired him and helped him to shape his own educational background and philosophy of education.

CHAPTER I

François Rabelais

1490 (?) - 1553

For France, the fifteenth century was a period of turmoil, acute ecclesiastical, hierarchical controversies—the Great Schism—and the bloody century of the Hundred Years' War. Nevertheless this was the time when the dawn of the Renaissance was beginning to send forth its stream of light from Italy into the different parts of Europe. The sixteenth century, on the other hand for France was a period of great prosperity[1] —people full of hope, abundant crops, the light of a new life invigorating and illuminating a number of keen intellects. Here and there, one would find a shining constellation of ecclesiastical and political leaders, encouraging, supporting and protecting under their wings the soarings of a select group of curious and independent souls aspiring at an intellectual, moral and religious freedom. It is true, that even during this century, life was not easy, nor was it safe for the daring minds seeking truth, abundant life and freedom. Already the number of such persons was on the increase. And, as the forces of darkness, tradi-

---

[1]Cf. **François Rabelais,** Tout ce qui existe de ses oeuvres: par Louis Moland. p. IX.

tionalism, formalism and absolutism presented a united front, these numerically very small vanguards of enlightenment, reawakening, activity and freedom, in their turn, formed a sort of secret intellectual brotherhood.

Chief among these rebellious intellects was François Rabelais. Though he did not possess the ardent fervor of a martyr for a great cause, but through the fertility, and resourcefulness of his mind, the suppleness of his personality, and through a keen sense of a real practical man, he successfully managed to ridicule the abuses of the church, the formalism of scholastic education, the narrowness of monastic life, the shortcomings of the courts. In short, anything and everything that embodied the spirit of medievalism was subjected to his stinging and biting satire, in which he was a master, par excellence, and this was done at a time when such things were summarily dealt with by the punishment of death. Rabelais' personality is extremely interesting. Was he a frolicking, jovial and mirthful man, who exercised his pen, without any serious aim, merely to amuse his contemporaries with his satire? Or, was he a serious-minded individual who had a new message to give to his compatriots, the message of a new life, the spirit of humanism, the exaltation of the life here below, a love for nature and the beauties of living in freedom, emancipated from the shackles of intellectual and spiritual servitude of a formal, shallow, insincere and degenerated type of life, left as an heritage from the darkness of the Middle ages? Was he either one or the other? It is indeed difficult to answer this question. Everything is shrouded in mystery about Rabelais. Even his biography is full of gaps, fabulous tales and inconsistencies. He is an enigmatic figure. "Nothing, probably is factitious about Rabelais, nothing is sham, neither his wisdom, nor his folly. He represents an enigmatic nature, a strange character, a genius apart in itself, exuberant and cautious at the same time, bizarre and sensible, dissolute and judicious, with prodigious faculties, and with remarkable loftiness of thought and fits of intemperate gayety which nothing can stop."[1] Rabelais himself has felt the need of elucidating the minds of his readers in this regard. For he writes: "But it is not suitable to estimate the works of men with such lightness. There is a saying to the effect that, the habit does not make the monk—namely, the materials treated here are not wanton (folastre) as the title would pretend them to be."[2] Most critics incline to believe that, although his pur-

---
[1] Cf. **François Rabelais,** La Vie de Rabelais, par Louis Moland p. XXXVIII.
[2] Cf. Prologue, Gargantua.

pose was serious in attempting to satirize the abuses which he saw all around him, he was cautious enough to soften the effects of his biting sarcasm, by resorting to buffoonery. By nature, he was well-fitted for this type of work. In this, he represents the jovial spirit of his age.

"It is better to write of laughter than of tears,
Because laughter is proper to man.
Live joyously."[1]

Another trait that characterized him markedly was his burning zeal and love for learning. As a representative of this age of awakening he tried to quench his thirst for information by drinking at the fountain-head of knowledge wherever he went. Continuous travel, from city to city, country to country, and endless shifting of position from one monastic order to another has been an efficacious means for satisfying his inexhaustible intellectual curiosity. Thus, he learned several languages: Latin, Greek, Hebrew, Arabic, Italian, Spanish, etc. He mastered medical science, anatomy, archaeology, music, botany and poetry. "François Rabelais gathered a knowledge which caused astonishment to his most learned contemporaries. He became philosopher, mathematician, jurisconsult, musician, arithme-

---

[1]Cf. Mieux est de ris que de larmes escrire
Pour ce que rire est de propre de l'homme.
    Vivez joyeux.—In the verse addressed to the Readers (Aux Lecteurs).

tician, geometrician, astronomer, painter and poet. In this, he equalled Erasmus and Budaeus. But the thing in which he was unique or astonishingly rare during his century, is the fact that his knowledge was not only that of books. It was knowledge gathered from nature, knowledge of spirit rather than that of letter, not only of words but of things, in short, living knowledge."[1] In this type of pansophic knowledge, both of books and of things, Rabelais was the best representative of French humanism and sense realism.

Again, a love of nature and a fondness of the joy of life was another striking characteristic of François Rabelais. In contrast to the narrow life of his confreres within the walls of monasteries, and in utter opposition to the barren and narrow life of schoolmen during the Middle ages, Rebelais lived a restless life, full of temptations, diversions, abundance and also crudeness, in pursuit of learning, joy, happiness, and experiences:

"He loved life more abundantly, more supremely than anyone of his ancestors or intellectual descendants, as one only could love life in this century and at this epoch of the century, during the first and magnificent expansion of unbridled humanism, which wants to have everything at once and together, everything without any measure— to know, to feel and to act. Rabelais loved life not by a system or abstraction, but by an instinct, by all his senses

[1] Cf. **Oeuvres Complètes Illustrées** de Anatole France, fitte, pp. 34-35. Colmann-Lévy-Editeurs, Paris, 1928. Tome XVII. **Rabelais.** August Compte, Pierre Laf-

and all his soul, not merely an idea of life, not certain forms of life, but the concrete and visible life, the life of the living beings, the life of flesh and the life of the spirit, all forms, beautiful and ugly, all acts, noble or vulgar, in which life found an expression. From this life flow his writings."[1]

It is easy to understand how the newly emancipated souls during the period of the Renaissance could fall into the extreme adoration of nature and life, in contrast to the extreme abnegation of these things by the ascetic schoolmen of the Dark ages.

Rabelais also abhorred everything that savored of intolerance. A love of humanity dominated his heart. This love for toleration was beginning to express itself in a century when people were persecuted savagely for their beliefs and ideas. Rabelais felt the stings of intolerance on his own person. He observed how his friends were pursued for their faith. 1545 is the year of the massacres of Merindol, Coste and Cabrières under François I. In 1543 Robert Estienne, celebrated humanist publisher, and Marot, the poet, escaped persecutions by fleeing from France. In 1546 Etienne Dolet, the famous humanist scholar, was hanged and burned. Rabelais himself was saved from annihilation through the powerful protection of his influential patrons, whom he

---
[1] Cf. **Histoire de La Littérature Française**, G. Lanson, p. 255.

had wisely chosen—such men as Cardinal du Bellay, Bishop Geoffroy d'Estissac, Chatillon, and even the King François I and Henry II. Rabelais showed his infinite resourcefulness by taking refuge under the protecting wings of these men. Consequently, he did not desist from fiercely ridiculing men of influence for their abuses and pretensions, thereby rendering a great service for the acceleration of social reforms.

Biography of Rabelais.—Rabelais was born at Chinon, in the province of Touraine, famous for its great men of imagination and creative genius. the date of his birth is disputed. Most authorities agree on 1490. His father was either an innkeeper, an apothecary or a proprietor of a small vineyard. He desired that his son should enter a monastic order. Thus, François Rabelais studied in the Benedictine abbey of Souillé, then at the convent of Baumette, near Angers, under the order of the Cordeliers. Here he met Geoffroy d'Estissac, who later on became bishop of Maillezais and an influential patron of Rabelais. Through him François entered the abbey of the Fonteney-Le-Compte, of the order of the Cordeliers. Here he completed his novitiate and was ordained a priest. But, Rabelais was a lover of ancient Greek and the Cordeliers did not favor the study of pagan authors. A few fanatic monks found certain Greek books in the cell of Rabelais, for which he suffered much. Rabelais left the Cordeliers and found a way to enter, in 1523, the Benedictine abbey of Legugé. He did not like this place either, and in 1525 took the garb of a secular priest and began his endless travels. In 1530 he attended the University of Montpellier and received his bachelor's degree in medicine inside of three months. From 1532-1533 he was attached to the hospital at Lyons as a medical doctor with a salary. There he began to publish his books. In this study we are concerned chiefly with "Gargantua" and "The Heroic Deeds of Pantagruel." Then he went to Rome as medical advisor to Cardinal Jean du Bellay in 1533, again in 1536, and in 1538. In Rome he learned Arabic from a Greek scholar, and studied archaeology, and botany. In 1537 he again entered Mountpellier and received the advanced degrees of Licencié and Doctor of Medicine. In 1545 he received the privilege to publish his third book, the second book of Pantagruel. After the death of Francois I and upon the execution of Etienne Dolet, he took refuge at Metz where he practiced medicine. Then, with his proctector Cardinal du Bellay, in 1551 he returned once more to France, and obtained the curate of Meudon and Saint-Christophe-du Jambet which he resigned later. There he published his fourth book and died in April 1553. His fifth book was published ten years after his death. Sorbonne opposed especially his third and fourth books. His works were condemned, but Rabelais published them, nevertheless, through his resourcefulness.

Gargantua and Pantagruel are not essays on education. They are fantastic tales, full of seriousness and buffoonery, biting sarcasm, and profound wisdom. The persons of the tale, imaginary giants, represent real personages of French society of that period; some of them are pure inventions of the author. Through them Rabelais expounds his theory on learning, education, religion, morals and life. Words flow as torrents from the pen of this great master of French language —archaic in its form, the French of the sixteenth century. The "Gargantua and Pantagruel" consist of five books, the first one devoted to the description of the "Horrific Life of the Great Gargantua, Father of Pantagruel" and the remainder of the books devoted to the "Heroic Deeds and Sayings of The Good Pantagruel." The chapters which interest us are those in which the author's educational ideas are expounded—Book I, chapters XIV, XV, XXI, XXII, XXIV; Book II, chapters V, VI, VII, VIII.

Educational Ideas of Rabelais.— Rabelais with his characteristic style satirizes and ridicules the old scholastic education. "Gargantua" contains mostly his destructive criticism directed at the formalism, absurdity and ineffectiveness of the scholastic education. In "Pantagruel," chapter VIII, we find his constructive ideas upon which he believes the new education should be based.

Grandgousier, a giant, and an imaginary king, had a son, whom he called Gargantua. He wished his son to be brought up in the best manner possible. For this reason he hired a tutor, named Master Thubal Holofernes, who taught Gargantua his A,B,C,'s so well, that he could say them by heart backwards. The child was five years three months old. Later Master Holofernes gave Gargantua as text-books, "Donat," "Le Facet," "Theodelet" and "Alanus in Parabolis." The pupil was by this time thirteen years six months and two weeks old. Fortunately or unfortunately Master Holofernes died. In his place, a new teacher was hired, Master Jobelin Bridé, a "coughing fellow" or a "muzzled dolt," who gave Gargantua to read a series of old Latin books, among them, a book called "Dormi Secure." This was a compilation of ready-made sermons for the use of preachers who wished "to sleep soundly" rather than undergo the trouble of preparing

original sermons. In spite of the fact that the
teacher labored hard to teach and the pupil struggled hard to learn, Grandgousier noticed that his
son "did nevertheless profit nothing, but which is
worse, he grew thereby foolish, simple, doted and
blockish." Consequently he asked advice from
one of his friends Don Philip des Marays, who
told him that there are newer and better methods
of education. To prove this, a young man called
Eudemon, trained in this new learning, was
brought before Grandgousier. The young man
attracted the attention and admiration of the
giant king for the elegance of his manners, for
the fluency and effectiveness of his speech. At
the side of this young man Gargantua was abashed and could do nothing but "to shed tears like
a cow." The tutor of Eudemon, Master Ponocrates, was hired in order to teach Gargantua. The
new teacher, his pupil, and a retinue of pages were
sent to Paris "to find out what was the study of
the young men of France at that time." At Paris
they observed at close range the sophistry of
schoolmen still clinging tightly to the old methods of scholasticism. Ponacrates first observed
the behavior of his pupil, and permitted him to
do as he pleased, knowing full well "that nature
cannot stand sudden changes without great violence." He called a doctor who "purged him
canonically with anticyrian hellebore, by which

he cleansed all the alteration, corruption and perverse habits of his brain. By this means also Ponocrates made him forget all that he had learned under his old teachers. To do this better they brought him into the company of learned men, in whose imitation he had a great desire and affection to study and amount to something. Afterwards he put himself into such a way of studying that he lost not a single hour in the day, but employed all his time in learning and honest knowledge. Gargantua used to wake up about four o'clock in the morning. While they were rubbing him, they read to him some pages of Divine Scripture, aloud and clearly, with a pronunciation fit for the matter. Then he oftentimes gave himself to worship, adore, pray and send up his supplication to God. Then he went into the secret places to obey a call of his natural digestions. There his master repeated what had been read, explaining to him the most obscure and difficult points. In returning, they observed the sky, if it was such as they had seen it the preceding night, and into what signs the sun was entering and also the moon for that day. This done, he was dressed, combed, curled, trimmed and perfumed, during which time they repeated to him the lessons of the day before. He himself said them by heart, and upon them would found some practical cases, concerning the estate of man.

Sometimes this would take three hours, but generally they ceased as soon as he was all dressed. Then for three hours a lecture was read to him. This done, they went out, always discussing about the lecture, into a field called Brack or into the meadows where they played ball, long-tennis, and pile trigon, gallantly exercising their bodies as before they had exercised their minds. All their play was in liberty, for they left their game when they wished, and generally they quit playing when their bodies were in perspiration or when they were otherwise tired. Then they were well wiped and rubbed, changed their shirts, and walking softly, they went to see if dinner was ready. There, while waiting, they recited clearly and eloquently certain sentences that they had retained of the lecture. However, Master appetite came and then they sat down at the table. At the beginning of the dinner, there was read some pleasant stories about the valor of the ancient times, until he had taken his wine. Then, if they thought it good, they continued the lecture or began to discourse joyously together, speaking first of the virtue, propriety, efficacy and nature of all that was served at the table. By means of which he learned in a little time all the passages suitable for this, that were found in Pliny, Athenaeus, Dioscorides, Julius Pollux, Galen, Porphyrious, Oppians, Polybius, Heliodore, Aristotle,

Oelian and others. He learned so well the passages from these, that in that time there was not a physician that knew half so much as he did. After using tooth picks and thanking God, they brought cards, not to play, but to learn a thousand fine tricks and new inventions, which were all taken out of arithmetic. By this means he fell in love with that numerical science, and every day after dinner and supper he passed his time with it as he used to do at cards and dice. He knew so much of it, both in theory and practice, that Tunsal, the Englishman, who had written amply in it, confessed that really, in comparison to him, he did not know much in it; and not only in that, but in other mathematical sciences, such as geometry, astronomy and music.—As to musical instruments he learned how to play upon the lute, the virginals, the harp, the German flute with nine holes, the viol and the sackbut.—After this, he worked three hours at his principal studies. Then they went out with a young gentleman of Touraine, the Esquire Gymnast, who taught him the art of riding." The author describes here how he rode all kinds of horses and how he excelled in all kinds of tricks in this. "Then he tossed the pike, played with the two-handed sword —etc. Then he would hunt the hart, the roebuck, the bear, the fallow deer, the wild boar, the hare, the pheasant, the partridge, etc. . . He wrestled, ran, jumped—at one leap he would skip over a ditch, spring over a hedge—He swam in deep waters on his belly, on his back, sideways, with all his body etc.—Coming out of the water, he ran furiously up against a hill and with the same rapidity and swiftness ran down again. He climbed up trees like a cat, leaped from one to the other like a squirrel.—He cast the dart, threw the bar, put the stone, practiced the javelin.— Then he lifted from the ground two great weights of lead (saulmones de plomb) each of them weighing eight thousand and seven hundred quintals.— And after using his time like this, and being rubbed, washed and refreshed by new clothes, he returned softly and passing through certain meadows or other grassy places, observed trees and plants, comparing them with what is written of them in the books of the ancients, and took with him to his house handfuls of them, where a young page had charge of them—together with all instruments requisite for herborising.—To exercise his lungs he shouted very loudly.—Returning to the house, while supper was being prepared, they repeated certain passages of that which had been read, and sat down at table. . . After eating a hearty supper . . . he gave himself to singing and playing on harmonious instruments, or otherwise passed his time at some sports, made with cards or dice. . . There they remained some nights frolicking thus and making themselves merry till it was time to go to bed; and sometimes they visited learned men or men who had been in foreign countries. . . Before going to bed they again went out to observe the skies and reviewing that which he had read, seen, learned, done and understood during the whole day, and praying to God they went to bed.

"—On rainy days they would follow the same program in a nice warm room, until noon, but after dinner, instead of their customary exercises, they would stay indoors and by way of apotherapy, to make their bodies healthful, they passed their time in making bundles of hay, in cleaving and sawing of wood and in threshing sheaves of corn at the barn. They studied painting and sculpture. . . They went also to see the drawing of metals, or the casting of artillery, or they went to see how the lapidaries, goldsmiths and cutters of precious stones worked, or they visited the alchymists, money-coiners, watch-makers, looking-glass-framers, printers, organists, dyers, and other workers, and everywhere giving them a little wine, they learned and observed the industry and invention of the trades. Then they went also to hear lectures, the solemn arts, repetitions, declamations, the pleadings of gentle lawyers, the sermons of evangelical preachers. . . and instead of herborizing, they visited the stores of druggists, herbalists and apothecaries, and carefully observed fruits, roots, leaves, gums, seeds, the grease and ointments of some foreign countries, and also how they adulterated them. He went to see the jugglers, tumblers, mountebanks, and observed their cunning, their somersaults. Upon their return, they ate more soberly at supper. . .that they might not be incommodated for lack of their usual physical exercise."

Thus Gargantua was trained with good discipline, full of judgment. His teacher provided for him also once in a month on a clear day an outing, either towards Gentilly, or Boulogne, or to Montrouge or Charanton bridge, or to Vanves, or to St. Cloud, and there they spent the whole day in sporting, merry-making, drinking healths, playing, singing, dancing, tumbling in some meadow. "But although that day was passed without books or lecture, it was not spent without profit; for in those meadows they usually repeated certain pleasant verses from Virgil's agriculture, from Hesiod, or from Politian's husbandry, etc." Here we have at length quoted from chapters XXIII and XXIV of Gargantua,[1] trying to be as faithful to the original as possible and, at times condens-

---

[1] Cf. Chapter XXIII and XXIV; either in **François Rabelais**, Tout ce qui existe de ses oeuvres, par Louis Moland, or a selected edition in English, by Adolph Cohn and prepared by Curtis Hidden Page. G. P. Putnam Sons, New York, N. Y.

ing and summarizing the thoughts of Rabelais. It must be at once granted that this educational program is to suit the capacities of a giant. But discounting the exaggeration, and analyzing it carefully the reader will be convinced that Rabelais is an advocate of a realistic education.

I. Education Through Real Things.—Rabelais, condemning the bookishness of the old scholastic education, proposed in its place an education that is based both on book knowledge as well as practical experience. He did not despise words but he stressed the need of supplementing these with actual observations of things. In Rabelais' work we find the beginnings of object teaching, which finally was to find its culmination in the teaching of sciences. Rabelais proved to be an experimentalist, at least in the anatomical science. While he was attached to the hospital at Lyons, he gave a public demonstration, dissecting the body of a hanged criminal.

II. Physical Education.—While emphasizing the importance of erudition even to an extreme degree, Rabelais stressed again and again the necessity of developing the body, through all sorts of physical exercises. He was a doctor of medicine by profession. On the health of the body he had some very sane views. He showed the importance of personal hygiene—cleanliness, washing, bathing, moderation of diet and adapting the diet to the occupation and the particular need of the individual in question. There is, really, some novelty in his plan of taking Gargantua once a month to some nearby meadow where he is allowed to play in freedom, enjoy all types of outdoor sports, thereby developing a better appetite for further intellectual work.

III. School Excursions.—Rabelais, to supplement the knowledge of Gargantua gathered from books, pointed out the need of taking him to factories, shops, meetings, court-houses and various other places, where he would be able to observe and to gain first-hand knowledge of meaningful activities of life. Rabelais must have observed the utter isolation of the scholastic or monastic school from life and society. Therefore, he believed that through these excursions the artificial gap existing between education and life could be spanned. In this regard, he was the most modern of all modern educators.

IV. Pleasant Methods—He was an advocate of strenuous discipline, voracious reading, and unbounded learning. Yet, he pointed out the need of a more pleasant and agreeable method of teaching reading, arithmetic, geometry, etc. While playing cards, the pupil became interested in these studies. Perhaps he had not a full comprehension of the psychological fact that the more genuinely one is interested in a given activity the more willing he is to take pains. For this type of genuine interest the artificial means of plays, dices and games are not needed. Yet the pleasanter method of approaching the subject-matter as advocated by Rabelais is much better than the old medieval idea of force, rods, extraneous punishments and rewards.

Again, the method of approach in the scheme of Rabelais' education is the informal rather than the formal. Through his own experience he had, no doubt, discovered that where one could take advantage of the informal method of learning one should do so. He himself had learned through this informal method several foreign languages and all kinds of sciences known to his contemporaries.

V. Religious and Moral Education.—Rabelais, one of the greatest mockers of ecclesiastical formalism, who was persecuted for his new ideas, was not opposed to religious and moral education. On the contrary, he advocated the need of religious and moral training of a genuine type—religion without hypocrisy, intolerance, pretension, and verbalism. "But because as the wise Solomon said, 'Wisdom entereth not into a malicious mind' and that science without conscience is but the ruin of the soul; it behooveth thee to serve, to love, to fear God, and on Him to lay all thy thoughts and all thy hope, and by faith formed in and through charity, to cleave unto Him so that thou mayest never go away from Him by thy sins."[1] In spite of the grossness, crudities, and buffoonery that we find in his works, one will also find a seriousness of purpose and a goodness of spirit.

VI. **Nature good, hence Freedom.**—At the time, when Rabelais lived, both Roman and as well Lutheran and Calvinistic creeds believed in the natural depravity of the child. Rabelais in reaction to this fatalistic view preached the doctrine of the goodness of nature. In describing the life as it existed in the abbey of Theleme, the creation of his own imagination, he made this remark: "Men that are free, well-born, well-bred, and conversant in honest companies, have naturally an instinct and spur that pushes them into virtuous actions, and draws them away from vice."[2] Again, for the motto of Thelemites, he gave the

---

[1] Cf. **Pantagruel,** Chapter VIII. ("Mais, parce que, selon le Sage Salomon, sapience n'entre point en ame malivole, et science sans conscience n'est que ruine de l'ame, il te convient servir, aimer at craindre Dieu, et en lui mettre toutes tes pensées et tout ton espoir; et par foy formée de charité, estre a luy adjoinct, en sorte que jamais n'en sois desemparé par peché.")

[2] Cf. **Gargantua,** chapter LVII.

following dangerous rule: "Fais ce que vouldras," (Do as thou wilt). As a reaction to the intellectual, religious, moral, social and political absolutism of the Middle Ages, this extreme doctrine is a natural one, but it is evident that it is dangerous and utopian. This served its purpose, however, in influencing the minds of his contemporaries for the bringing about of an era free from the shackles of absolutism which had deadened the spirit of creation and the intellectual development of the people of the Medieval world. Critics comment that Rabelais' idea of freedom was not that of licentious and unbridled type, but rather that of the disciplined.

VII. Encyclopedic Knowledge.—Freed from the deep ignorance of the Dark Ages leaders of humanism during the sixteenth and seventeenth centuries advocated learning anything and everything that could be learned. Rabelais personally stored an almost inexhaustible amount of knowledge in languages, theology, astronomy, botany, medicine, arithmetic, geometry, and music. It is natural that he should advocate an encyclopedic type of knowledge for Gargantua and Pantagruel:

"For this reason, I admonish you to use your young age to take advantage of studies and virtues. . . . I intend and desire that you should learn the languages perfectly. First the Greek, as Quintillian would have it; secondly the Latin; and then the Hebrew for the Holy

Scripture; and then the Chaldee and Arabic similarly, and that you should form your style, in imitation of Plato; as for the Latin, after Cicero. Let there be no history which you will not have ready in your memory, for which cosmography will help you much. Of the liberal arts of geometry, arithmetic and music, I gave you a taste when you were little, five or six years old; continue further in them. Study all the rules of astronomy. Omit divining astrology and the art of Lullius, as abuses and vanities. I would have you to know by heart the good texts of the civil law and then confer them with philosophy.

As for the knowledge of the facts of nature, I would have you to study them with curiosity; and that there be no sea, river, nor fountain of which you do not know the fishes; all the birds of the air; all the trees, shrubs, whether in forests or orchards; all the herbs of the earth; all the metals that are hidden within the bowels of the earth; all the precious stones of the orient and of the south; let all of these be not unknown to you. Then peruse most carefully the books of Greek, Arabian and Latin physicians, without condemning the Talmudists and Cabalists; and by frequent anatomy acquire perfect knowledge of the other world, which is man. And at some hours of the day, begin to study the Holy Scriptures. The New Testament and the Epistles of the Apostles in Greek; and then the Old Testament, in Hebrew. In short, let me see you a bottomless pit of knowledge: for from now on as you grow and become a man, you must leave this tranquility and rest of study and you must learn chivalry and warfare, in order to defend my house and to help our friends in all their affairs against the assaults of malefactors. In brief, I wish that you test how much you have profited, which you could not do any better than by publicly maintaining theses and conclusions in all knowledge against all, and haunting the company of learned men both in Paris and elsewhere!"[1]

---

[1] Cf. **Pantagruel**, Chapter VIII. The famous letter which Pantagruel received, while at Paris, from his father, Gargantua. This letter is worth reading many times. It shows the fervent Christian faith of Rabelais.

In this quotation the curriculum of a pansophic and humanistic type of education is described by Rabelais. It embraces all sorts of information. The aim is to make the student "a bottomless pit of knowledge." This aim was to be further emphasized during the seventeenth century by Comenius. It is superfluous to comment that it is an impossible aim to attain, and one which, if carried to its logical conclusion, will produce the so-called walking encyclopedias who are apt not to have judgment, originality in thinking, and willingness and ability in action. Even though Rabelais had very sagaciously observed the importance of learning by doing and experiencing, yet he has not been able to avoid laying too much stress on cramming the mind with all sorts of knowledge for its own sake and not for the sake of its functional value for the individual. However, it is not justifiable to expect that this criterion of the functional value of information should have entered the mind of a man, who by nature was very curious, possessed an enormous amount of intellectual capacity and lived in a century when one's reputation as an educated person was measured by the copiousness of passages which he could cite in an impromptu fashion out of a well-filled memory.

In summing up the educational influences of Rabelais, we are justified in ranking him as one of the foremost educational theorists of the sixteenth century, because of the marvellously complete educational scheme which he left to us in his writings; furthermore, because of the influence which he exercised upon the educational thoughts of Montaigne, John Locke and Rousseau. A very enthusiastic British critic goes perhaps further than we would be willing to go in evaluating the educational influence of Rabelais:

"When we consider Rabelais' scheme in its entirety we may feel that in originality, extent, in balanced appreciation of everything really worthy of inclusion in an educational system, it far transcends the recommendations and practice of all the rest of the humanist educators, even perhaps of the greatest schoolmaster among them, Vittorino Da Feltre himself. That Rabelais has received such scant justice from the general public as a pedagogic theorist, may perhaps be accounted for partly by the fact that the educational chapters form such a small proportion of the whole, and that for most people, the whole has a very different interest. But it may be equally true that his coarseness has limited his real audience so that many people have talked of him on hearsay without really knowing him and as a natural consequence have talked quite inadequately."[1]

M. Jean Fleury in his work on Ralebais praises the author of the "Gargantua and Pantagruel" by citing the case of two historically famous French teachers, Bossuet and Fénelon,[2] who respectively had charge of the education of the

[1] Cf. **Studies in French Education.** Geraldine Hodgson, p. 17, Cambridge University Press.
[2] Cf. Our chapter on Fénelon.

Dauphin and the grandson of Louis XIV. Bossuet was entrusted with the training of the Dauphin. Fénelon had the responsibility of the education of the Duke of Burgundy. Bossuet followed the scholastic method of stern discipline, commands, memorization and direct preaching like our master Jobelin of Gargantua. Fénelon took advantage of the method employed by Ponocrates. The pupil of Bossuet turned out to be a "deplorable mediocrity," whereas the pupil of Fénelon "grew in intelligence, became transformed morally." While Mr. Fleury admits that perhaps the natural endowment of the two princes had something to do with this educational result —the failure of Bossuet and the success of Fénelon, yet he rather believes that the difference of the two opposing systems of education was the prime cause in producing this result. Thus, M. Fleury ascribes Fénelon's success as a tutor of the Duke of Burgundy to the educational system of Ponocrates, the creation of Rabelais. It might perhaps be added that the differences in the personalities of the two famous teachers, Bossuet and Fénelon, should be taken into account. Fénelon,[1] because of his infinite kindness, love and

---

[1]Cf. "Très bon, du reste, du fond du coeur, infiniment serviable, bienfaisant en prélat, magnifique en grand seigneur, et charitable en saint, il a pratiqué toutes les méthodes de l'art de donner avec grace." XVIIe Siècle, **Etudes Littéraires**, p. 340, E. Faguet.

sympathy, tact and imagination possessed qualities requisite for an artist-teacher, whereas Bossuet lacked some of these qualities. By making this remark we are not inclined to belittle the great contributions which Rabelais made in the field of humanistic education. He sowed the seeds; the eighteenth century educational philosophers harvested the crop in full maturation.

CHAPTER II

Michel Eyquem de Montaigne

1533 - 1592

Among the shining luminaries who illumined the intellectual horizon of the world after mankind emerged out of the gloomy darkness of the Middle Ages, Montaigne occupied a place of honor. He was a humanist thoroughly versed in the classical literature of the Greeks and Romans. He embodied the spirit of his age, a scorn for everything that savored of dogmatism, irrationalism, and supernaturalism. He was a skeptic, although he had at least a faith in man and in the goodness of nature. His skepticism, epitomized in "Que sais-je?" (What do I know?) was a natural outgrowth of his desire to extricate himself from the complicated tangles of the religious dogmatism of his times and the bloody intolerance which set the world afire with its all-embracing flames. Gustave Lanson explains this evident skepticism of Montaigne in the following passage: "—I well believe that his transcendental skepticism aims at cutting the roots of those metaphysical affirmations from which our social life takes its form, and for which we cut the throats of one another . . . what does this mean except that Montaigne gives his skepticism as a remedy for fanaticism? That is all, nothing more nor less."[1]

Michel de Montaigne, the great essayist, moralist, and educational theorist of the sixteenth century desired to enjoy a life of peace, ease, and leisure free from outburst of extreme passions. He preached social virtues, simplicity, sincerity, loyalty, truthfulness, moderation and temperance. In almost all of his essays one finds a reference to these virtues, the qualifications of the honest gentleman, the ideal man of Montaigne. Among his several essays, condensed in three books, without any methodic plan, the following are of importance for teachers who wish to understand Montaigne and his educational and social philosophy. Book I, chapters 24 and 25 deal more specifically with the problems of education with which we are concerned here. Book I, chapter 27 discusses "Friendship: book II, chapter 1, the problem of "The Inconstancy of our Actions," book II, chapter 8, "On the Affections of Fathers to their Children," and chapter 17, "Of Presumption," contains important points on his autobiography. Book II, chapter 29 treats of "Virtue;" book II, chapter 36 of "The Worthiest and Most Excellent Men." Book III, chapter 3 contains very impor-

---

[1] Cf. **Histoire de La Littérature Française**, G. Lanson, p. 329.

tant information on his character, personality, and love for books. Quoting from Florio, the first translator of the Essays, we see the intimate life of Montaigne. "At home I betake me somewhat the oftner to my library, whence all at once I command and survey all my household. It is seated in the chiefe entrie of my house, thence I behold under me my garden, my base court, my yard, and look even into most rooms of my house. There without order, without method, and by peece-meales I turne over and ransacke, now one booke and now another. Sometimes I muse and rave; and walking up and downe I endight and enrijister these my humours, these my conceits. It is placed on the third storie of a tower." Book III, chapter 8 treats of "The Art of Conferring;" and chapter 10, "How One Ought to Govern his Will;" chapter 13, of "Experience."

A careful perusal of these and also other essays will reveal the trends of Montaigne's thoughts. He not only is a skeptic but an epicurean and egotist.[1] He loved his children only after they grew and became amiable and lovely. He had no place in his mind nor in his conduct for self-sacrifice as a virtue. Yet that is one of the highest virtues of a perfect man, the Christian

---

[1]Cf. Book III, 10. (Mon opinion est qu'il se fault prester, à aultruy et ne se donner qu'à soy mesme).

virtue, par excellence. There is a spirit of dilettantism in his writings. He lacks intellectual breath, although he touches "the skirts of all the hills" of human thought. Unlike Rabelais "who overdrives the mind and body" in his plan of education, Montaigne advocates moderation.

He was not interested in metaphysics. His chief interest was in ethics, morals and human psychology. His essays are written in his quiet library room, in solitude and tranquility, with a desire to portray his own self. Addressing the readers of his book, he says: "I desire to be seen in it in my own simple, ordinary and genuine fashion without artifice or study; for it is myself that I am portraying."[1] Introspection is his method of self-analysis. By portraying himself, however, he portrayed human nature, as Voltaire put it; as such his Essays deserve especial consideration.

Biography[2] **of M o n t a i g n e.**— Michel Eyquem de Montaigne was born in the castle of Montaigne, at Périgord, February 28, 1533. His ancestors were good business men; they engaged in commerce and became rich. His father, Pierre Eyquem, was born in this castle, abandoned business, fought in Italy and married a lady of Jewish

---

[1] Cf. **L'Auteur à Lecteur.** (car c'est moy que je peinds.)
[2] Cf. **Montaigne, par** Paul Stapfer, Hachette et Cie, Paris.

origin from Spain. He became counsellor and later mayor of Bordeaux. Michel de Montaigne received a very careful training, through the wise planning of his father. A German tutor was hired to teach him as soon as he was able to talk. As his tutor knew only German and Latin, Michel learned Latin in his childhood. He spoke Latin fluently at the age of six. He received his collegiate education at the College of Guyenne of Bordeaux. In this "prison of captive youth" (Book I, 25) he studied six years. He especially liked Latin poets, Ovid, Terence, Virgil. His teacher of literature was Marc-Antoine-Muret, one of the most celebrated Ciceronians of his times. Later, he graduated in law from the University of Toulouse. Among other public offices, he performed his duties as a member of the Parliament of Bordeaux and later as the mayor of the same city, with indifferent leisureliness. He married in 1565 and had six daughters, only one of whom lived. Upon the death of his rich father, in 1570, he retired from his public offices into his castle and devoted himself to study. When he was in Rome, he was elected to the office of the mayor of Bordeaux in 1581 and while he was the mayor of the city the great pestilence came and desolated the country, but Michel de Montaigne remained at Libourne and did not even preside at the election of his successor. This trait of selfishness of Montaigne has received much comment in French literature. From 1585-1592 Montaigne passed his life in isolation and devoted to reading, thinking and writing. He died in his castle in September 13, 1592, "Michel de Montaigne was sincere and even sufficiently modest. He had an adoration for the natural and for truth. He leaves with us an amiable memory and a sane impression of a perfectly honest man of a mediocre order."[1] During his life Montaigne had already published his Essays. But he had revised them for a new edition which was interrupted on account of his death. His complete works were published in 1595, three years after his death, by Mlle. de Gournay, his admirer and "sa fille d'alliance," with the supervision of the poet, Pierre de Brach, and also of his wife.

We are chiefly concerned with his educational thoughts condensed especially in Book I, chapters 24-25. The latter chapter was addressed to the Lady Diana of Foix, countess of Gurson, and it was entitled "Of the Institution and Education of Children." In this chapter one finds the germs of so many principles of modern education that it is a delight to analyze and point them out with due comments and interpretations.

---

[1] Cf. **Montaigne,** par Paul Stapfer, p. 194.

Educational Ideas of Montaigne.— There is no doubt that Rousseau received his inspiration and even some of his ideas from Montaigne as we shall point out later. John Locke also was no less influenced by this sixteenth century moralist and educational theorist. While Montaigne does not express his thoughts on educational matters in the same powerful rhetoric which characterizes the work of Rousseau, yet at times he hits happily at some statements which have become classic expressions of educational principles.

I. Education of the Whole Man.—Montaigne far from being satisfied with the old scholastic education which stuffed the mind of the scholars with half-understood dogmas and just as much discontented with the educational ideals and methods of the degenerated type of humanism, namely Ciceronianism, suggested that education should aim at the development of the whole man. He advocated the need of a liberal education. "I would have that the external decency of manners and the disposition of his personality be fashioned as well as his mind; for it is not a mind, it is not a body that we are going to erect, it is a man; we must not make two parts of him." (Book I, 25). He is opposed to the doctrine of the separation of the mind and the body. "Those who desire to part our two principal parts, and separate them from each other, are wrong. On the contrary, they must be recompleted and rejoined together." (Book II, 17). He sets forth as the aim of education one which was to be emphasized and reiterated by our own Dr. Edward L. Thorndike, "the good that comes out of our study, is to make us better and wiser." (Book I, 25). Again: "It seems to me that the first discourses with which his understanding must be sprinkled ought to be those that regulate his manners and his sense and teach him to know himself as well as to know how to die and how to live. Among the liberal arts, let us begin with the art that makes us free." (Ibid). Commenting about the futile aim of the pedants of his times in endeavoring to make grammarians and logicians out of their pupils, he says: "We on the contrary are seeking to form not a grammarian or a logician but a gentleman. Let us leave them to waste their time. We have more important tasks to perform." (Ibid). Let us compare this with the following statement of Rousseau to see how closely Rousseau follows Montaigne's line of thought: "On leaving my hands he will not, I admit, be a magistrate, a soldier, or a priest; first of all he will be a man." (Emile).

II. Education is not a Pouring-in Process.—Condemning the verbalistic education of his contemporaries and the vain efforts of teachers to impose their learning upon their pupils with forced discipline, he says: "Some (teachers) do not cease bawling as if they still were pouring in a funnel." (Book I, 25). Then he goes on discussing that the pupils are constantly required to repeat what they have been told by their teachers. He recommends that the tutors desist from doing this and give a chance to the pupil to develop a taste for every thing and permit him "to choose for himself, to discern for himself, sometimes paving the way for him and at times letting him open a path for himself. I would not have the teacher to invent and speak alone, but I wish him to allow his pupil to speak in his turn. . . It is good for the teacher to make his pupil trot before him to be better able to judge his pace and to decide to what degree he should stoop to fit himself to the strength of his pupil. For want of this proportion we spoil everything; and to know how to choose and how to act with moderation is one of the hardest tasks I know. It is a sign of a noble and strong spirit to know how to condescend to the childish ways of his pupil and how to guide them." (Book 1, 25). Let us compare this with the following beautiful statement of Ernst Von Wildenbruch, who put it in the mouth of a sympathetic modern German teacher: "Children are like flowers. They cannot come up to our level; we must stoop ourselves to them if we wish to know them."[1]

III. Training of the Judgment and Understanding.—Knowing full well that the Ciceronian pedants of his own days were well fed up with trivial knowledge but lacking in wisdom, Montaigne advocated developing the judgment and understanding of the pupil above everything else. To achieve this end he felt the need of a different type of teacher. For he says: "A child of noble parentage, who seeks learning not for the gain (because such an abject aim is unworthy of the grace and favor of the Muses, and besides has a regard of and dependence on others) and not so much for external convenience or ease but for his own and for enriching and adorning his inward mind, being desirous to succeed rather as an able man than as a learned man, I desire that the parents be careful in choosing for him a director whose head is well-made rather than filled well (La teste bien faicte que bien pleine). (Book I, 25). Exalting the importance of the understanding, he says: "It is our understanding said Epicharmus that sees and hears; it is the understanding that profits all and disposes all, that moves, dominates and rules all. Everything else

---
[1] Cf. **Kindertränen,** Ernst Von Wildenbruch, Henry Holt & Co., New York. "Kinder sind wie die Blumen, sie können nicht zu uns herauf, wir müssen uns zu ihnen niederbeugen, wenn wir sie erkennen wollen." p. 10.

is blind, deaf and without spirit. Really, we make him (our pupil) servile and coward not letting him do anything of himself." (Ibid). Again, "Plutarch rather would have people praise him for his judgment than for his knowledge." (Ibid). From the above passage it is evident that Montaigne understood the importance of self-activity for developing one's judgment and creative thinking.

IV. Memory Work Condemned. — While memory is important and especially to remember pertinent and well-connected facts is necessary for right judgment and creative thinking, yet the pernicious tendency of having children memorize abstract ideas without understanding them has resulted in developing human parrots. In the days of Montaigne an exaggerated significance was attributed to the latter type of memory work. As Heraclitus had proclaimed even six centuries before Christ, that "much learning does not teach sense," so Montaigne brings his indictment against the abominable practice of the pedants in stressing blind memorizing. He advises the tutor to avoid this error in his teaching: "Let him not ask his pupil to give an account of the words of his lesson, but rather of the meaning and substance; let him judge how much his pupil has profited by the lesson not by the testimony of his memory, but that of his life." (Book I, 25). He goes on emphasizing the need of correlation and application of facts learned by the pupil. "What the pupil has just learned let the teacher have him put in a hundred different shapes and fit it (correlate) to as many different subjects, to see if he has grasped it well and made it his own." (Ibid). Montaigne advises to cultivate independence of thought. After telling how people used to take the word of Aristotle as final on everything, he remarks: "Let the pupil sift everything and permit nothing to enter his head on mere authority and upon trust. Let the diversity of judgments be proposed to him; he will choose if he can; if not, he will remain in doubt." (Ibid). Here is his famous statement on memorizing without understanding: "To know by heart is not to know at all." (Sçavoir par coeur n'est pas sçavoir). (Ibid).

V. Learning by Doing.— To learn to swim one has to practice swimming. Likewise to learn to think one has to practice thinking. Montaigne expresses this idea in the following passage. "I would like to see Paluel and Pompey, these two good dancers of our times, teach us their tricks and high capers by just merely seeing them done, without having us move out of our places, as some teachers desire to train our understanding without any action or practice. Or, I should like to see anyone teach us to ride a horse, to toss a pike, to play upon the lute, or to sing without having us practice in these activities, as these teachers desire to teach us judging and speaking without providing us with any practice in judging and speaking. Everything that is presented to our eyes serves us as a sufficient book. In this apprenticeship type of learning, the roguish tricks of a page, the foolish act of a lackey, a talk made at the table are new subjects for us to consider." (Book I, 25). Again: "He who practices them profits better than he who merely knows them." (Ibid).

VI. Physical Exercise.— As Rabelais vigorously advocated the importance of physical exercise so did Montaigne. Referring to his pupil, he says: "It is not sufficient to make his mind strong; his muscles also must be strengthened." He goes on complaining how his own mind panted at times because it was attached to a delicate and sensitive body. He says: "I have seen men, women and children born with such a strong constitution that a beating with a cudgel hurts them less than a fillip (chiquenaude) would hurt me, and they did not budge neither their tongue, nor the eyebrows under the blows that they received. When the athletes copy (counterfeit) the philosophers' patience, it is the result of the vigor of their nerves (sinews) rather than that of their heart." (Book I, 25).

VII. The Place of Interest and Curiosity.— Montaigne placed a premium on interest and curiosity as a means of effective learning. He did not believe in teaching children lessons with force. "Let the tutor cultivate in his mind an honest curiosity to inquire[1] into everything; let him see everything that is singularly interesting around him, a building, a fountain, a man, the place of an ancient battle." (Book I, 25). Just like Rabelais, he too advocated the ineffective method of arousing interest, namely what we call sugar-coating. He believed that if the child learns his alphabet by games and dice, or his arithmetic through similar means, he will make a better headway than under pressure. Perhaps he will. But if a genuine interest, a zeal to learn and to know actuates the child, he will infinitely be better off. Hence it would be preferable to arouse this type of genuine interest through right motivation, in short, to psychologize the child's learning.

VIII. Harsh Discipline Condemned.— Montaigne, who was brought up in an excellent environment under the supervision of a fine tutor,

---

[1] Cf. **Democracy and Education,** John Dewey, MacMillan Co., "Acquiring is always secondary and instrumental to the act of inquiring." p. 173.

abhorred the harsh discipline that was in vogue in the schools of his times. He says: "To do all this, I would not have this young boy imprisoned and abandoned to the anger and melancholy humour of a furious schoolmaster; I would not have his spirit corrupted by keeping him in a hell-like place and at work, as some people do, fourteen or fifteen hours a day, as if he were a street-porter." (Book I, 25). Again: "This institution ought to be directed by a 'sweet-severe mildness' (une severe douleur), not as some people do, who instead of inviting children to the banquet of letters present them really with nothing but horror and cruelty. Away with this violence and force! For in my opinion there is nothing that bastardizes and stuns such a strong and well-born nature." (Ibid). He indicts the colleges of his times as real prisons of captive youth (vraye geaule de jeunesse captive). Does not the following passage sound like Rousseau? Speaking of college students, he says: "Meet them when they are going to their work you hear nothing but cries, both of children tormented and teachers drunk with anger. What a nice way to arouse the appetites of these young, tender and fearful souls for their lesson! What a fine way for guiding them with a frightful countenance and hands armed with whips! What a wicked and pernicious method! How much better it would be if their classes were strewn with flowers and foliages than with bloody birchen twigs! As the philosopher Speusippus did in his school, I would do likewise, namely portray The Joy, The Gladness, The Flora and The Graces in the school." (Ibid). He cautions the children not to devote an excessive amount of time to the study of books for "this makes them unfit for civil conversation and draws them away from better occupations." This admonition is rather negative and perhaps was well justified for the scholars of the sixteenth century.

IX. **Moral Education.**— Montaigne was a moralist. He was well-versed in the philosophy of ancient moralists. He stressed the importance of virtue as an aim in education. After setting forth the qualifications of an ideal tutor whose head is well-made rather than filled well, he adds: "I prefer morals, good behavior and understanding to mere knowledge." (Book I, 25). Again: "Let his conscience and virtue shine in his speech and his reason be his guide in his conduct." (Ibid). "He shall not so much repeat, as act his lessons. We must observe if there is prudence in his enterprises, if there is goodness and justice in his conduct, if there is judgment and grace in his speech, courage in his sickness, modesty in his plays, temperance in his pleasures, order in the management of his house." (Ibid). Speaking of simplicity he comments: "The speech that I like is the simple and naive speech, both in the mouth as well as on paper." (Ibid).

X. History and Languages.— Unlike Rousseau, Montaigne placed a great emphasis on the study of history. "In matters of books, history is my chief subject, and poetry which I like with a particular inclination." (Book 1, 25). He was interested especially in biographical history, since his chief interest was in forming his honest and virtuous gentleman. In his concept of the methods of teaching history, he was far advanced of his contemporaries. "He shall by the histories get acquainted with the best minds of centuries. This is a futile study for one who wishes it to be that way, but it is also a study replete with inestimable fruits for one who can make use of it and it is the only study, as Plato said, that the Lacedemonians reserved for themselves. What profit shall he not reap reading the 'Lives' of Plutarch? But the tutor should remember where his charge is tending. He should not so much impress in the mind of his pupil the date of the ruin of Carthage as the ways of Hannibal and Scipio; not so much where Marcellus died but why he was unworthy of his duty that he died there. Let him not teach him so much to know histories as to judge them." (Book I, 25).

As for the language teaching Montaigne expressed very progressive ideas. Even most of our modern foreign language teachers today would profit greatly if they should follow the method of teaching languages advocated by Montaigne. He tells his own experience about this. When he was able to speak, his father secured for him a German teacher who knew Latin but no French. Therefore Michel de Montaigne began to learn Latin and spoke it fluently when he was six years old. Even the household servants began to understand it. The famous Latinists were afraid to meet him for fear that their lack of profound knowledge might be revealed. He praises his teacher for his understanding and sympathy. Montaigne says that his teacher did not need to employ force to teach him. The lively interest and the consciousness of mastery day by day motivated him to go on with his studies. "Without art, without book, without grammar or precept, without rod and without tears" he had learned perfect Latin. In teaching this foreign language to Montaigne this excellent German teacher used psychological rather than logical[1] method, and it is not surprising that he succeeded well.

---

[1] Cf. **What is the Matter with the Teaching of Modern Languages?** K. A. Sarafian, **School and Society**, vol. 37, no. 959.

XI. The Importance of Travel.— Education received informally is futhered by travelling in foreign countries. Montaigne advises that the young traveller should observe and notice not the trivialities of the foreign customs, scenery or buildings but that he should observe the humours, mentality and spirit of other nations in order to compare theirs with them and to profit by this experience. "I would therefore have him begin travelling from his tender age to hit two marks with one stone, first to see a neighboring country whose language is far different from ours; for if one does not start very early one can not acquire the exact pronunciation of the foreign language . . ." (Book 1, 25). The importance of travel for mastery of a foreign language is today well understood by some of our educational institutions. For, they require a semester or more residence in the foreign country whose language one wishes to study, before they give the candidate a teacher's diploma in that language. The "New College" of Columbia University, recently established, even goes one step further in this matter. The residence and study in a foreign country is required not merely for the sake of mastery of foreign language but for the broadening of vision and sympathies of all prospective teachers majoring in other subjects than languages. Thus all the candidates for teaching are forced to meet this requirement. Rabelais, Montaigne and Rousseau stressed the importance of foreign travel since they themselves owed a great part of their learning and the broadening of their visions to their travels in Europe.

Montaigne also was convinced that education is not only received within the four walls of schools but almost everywhere. He says: "To our pupil a cabinet, a garden, the table and the bed, the solitude, a company, the morning and evening, all hours shall be alike, all places shall be a study for him. . . Thus our lesson, being passed over informally, without the strict requirements of time and place and connected with all our actions, will run unconsciously and smoothly; even the plays and exercises will be a part of his study—running, wrestling, music, dancing, hunting, horse-riding and managing of arms."

XII. World-Mindedness as an Aim.— To a man who was deeply steeped in ancient Greek and Roman literature and who had travelled in addition to his book learning, the vision of world brotherhood and world-mindedness would become almost a natural impulse. Thus, Montaigne laid a great stress on this broader outlook as an aim in education. "A marvellous clearness of man's judgment proceeds from an association in visiting the foreign countries (frequentation du monde). We are all constrained and heaped up and wrapped up in our own selves, and our vision is shortened by the length of our noses. People asked Socrates, whence he was; he did not answer of Athens, but of the world; he who had an imagination fuller and farther extending, embraced the universe as his city and extended his acquaintances, his company and his affections to all mankind." (Book 1, 25). Again: "This great world, which some multiply as species under one genus, is the mirror in which we must look in order to recognize ourselves in right bias. In short, I would have this world as the book for my pupil." (Ibid).

Concluding our comments after quoting so many passages from his Essays, we are justified in stating that Michel de Montaigne was one of the most important educational theorists of the sixteenth century. His general influence was great. Through the translation of his essays into English, by Florio in 1603, he exercised an influence on many British thinkers. Even Shakespeare quoted a passage from Montaigne in "The Tempest" and was influenced otherwise.[1] But

---

[1] Cf. **Shakespeare's Debt to Montaigne,** by George Coffin Taylor, Harvard University Press, Cambridge, Mass. "In almost every instance Shakespeare, before arriving at his destination, had made a detour through the forest of Montaigne." p. 27.

his greater influence is evidenced in the works of Fénelon, John Locke and especially Rousseau. If it had not been for Rousseau's powerful rhetoric, perhaps Montaigne's educational ideas would have fallen into oblivion. Montaigne is reproached, especially by French critics, for the fact that he does not give an important place for sheer effort[1] in his scheme of education. As we have commented before, the author of the interesting[2] essays was extremely opposed to restraint and to all kinds of extraneous efforts. "I condemn all kinds of violence in the education of a young soul, which one is bringing up to honor and freedom. There is a kind of servility in rigor and constraint; and I hold that what cannot be done by reason, by prudence and discretion, can never be achieved by force and compulsion." (Book II, 8). He exalted the importance of genuine curiosity and interest as the principal vehicle for the machinery of learning. In this, he belongs to the group of modern educators[3] who long ago cast

---

[1] Cf. **Histoire de la Littérature Française**, G. Lanson, p. 334. (Quel esprit, quelle volonté peuvent se former sans l'effort).

[2] Cf. "The sincerity and marrow of the man reaches to his sentence. I know not anywhere the book that seems less written. It is the language of conversation transferred to a book. Cut these words and they bleed; they are vascular and alive." **Representative Men**, by Emerson, p. 122. Hurst & Co. New York

[3] Cf. **Interest and Effort in Education**, by John Dewey, Houghton Mifflin Company, Boston, Mass.

aside the faculty psychology and the doctrine of formal discipline. On the other hand, one can reproach Montaigne for his inconsistencies, skepticism, epicureanism, dilettantism, and for his lack of self-sacrificing spirit. But in spite of all these, his enlightened judgment and penetrating observations on principles and methods of education constitute invaluable contributions, worthy of outright recognition. In his educational philosophy in his turn, Montaigne owed a great deal to Socrates, Plato, Cicero and Quintillian. But his basic judgments and decisions on important matters were products of his own creative thinking.

CHAPTER III

François Salagnac de la Mothe Fénelon

1651 - 1715

François Salagnac de la Mothe Fénelon occupies an important place in the history of French education as one of the founders of women's education. He not only contributed significant views on women's education but has exercised also his influence on the general theory of education, for it is evident that Jean-Jacques Rousseau was inspired with some of Fénelon's ideas in the formation of his own philosophy of education. Fénelon was not a mere speculaive theorist of education; he was one of the most successful teachers that the history of education has ever recorded. His personality, temperament, preferences, and infinite goodness, gentleness, affability of his character adapted him especially to the task of an "artist teacher" whom Vauvenargues in his imaginary dialogues proclaimed in the mouth of Bossuet, as a master teacher: "you were born to be the teacher of all the teachers of the world."

Critics of his literary work as well as of his educational writings are wont to draw a colorful picture of his captivating personality. Gustave Lanson summarizes his estimate of him in the following statement: "In all the works that I mentioned, and in all those that I omitted, the most interesting thing is this original, complex and captivating person."[1] Saint Simon, one of his contemporary critics, gives us the following portrait of Fénelon:

"This prelate was a big man, thin, well-built, with a large nose, eyes from which fire and intelligence burst forth like a torrent, a face the like of which I have never seen, one which is never forgotten after it has once been seen. In his face every feature was unified and the contrasts did not conflict with one another at all. It had graveness, galantry, seriousness. It bore out the doctor, the bishop, and the nobleman. One could read constantly on his face, thought, intelligence, gracefulness, decency, especially nobility. One needed to force himself to desist from looking at him."

Paul Janet, after quoting this portraiture of Fénelon, adds:

"One might say that the life and character of Fénelon and his very genius corresponded exactly to his external portrait; everything in him was unified and harmonized; the contrasts did not conflict with one another. Ancient and modern, Christian and secular, mystic and statesman, common and noble, gentle and headstrong, genial and subtle, captivating the 18th century as he had captivated the 17th, full of faith as much as a child, and bold as much as Spinoza, Fénelon is one of the most original figures which the Catholic church has produced."[2]

Gentleness, affableness, persuasiveness, an intense love for the beautiful in nature, in art and

---
[1] Cf. **Histoire de la Littérature Française**, Lanson, p. 616.
[2] Cf. **Fénelon**, par Paul Janet; p. 6.

in man, and a strong desire to mould the character of the young were the most outstanding traits of his personality, hence his success as a teacher.

Biography of Fénelon.—Fénelon was born in 1651 in a castle at Périgord. He came from a noble family and his feelings and sentiments were noble, par excellence. Religion attracted him particularly. Therefore he was sent to the Saint Sulpice Theological Seminary. Upon his graduation he was given charge of an institution, "Des Nouvelles Catholiques," where young Protestant girls converted to Catholicism were instructed and catechized in the faith of the church. Fénelon, through his affableness and persuasiveness, made a great success as the head of this institution. This also gave him practical experience in the study of human nature, and in the training of young girls. As a result of his first-hand observation, he wrote his first work, a discourse "On the Education of Girls."

In 1689 the Duke and Duchesse of Beauvilliers selected Fénelon as the teacher to train and educate the young Duke of Burgundy, the grandson of Louis XIV.

In the year 1693 Fénelon was admitted to the French Academy. Then, through the influence of Bossuet in 1695, he was appointed archbishop of Cambray. Here he was enjoying great popularity, but two important events brought disfavor upon him: the publication, against his will, of his pedagogical fiction, "Telemachus," 1699, and his entanglement in the controversy on the new religious doctrine, "Quiétisme." For this he was persecuted by Bossuet, and finally condemned by Rome for his defense of the "Quiétisme." Furthermore, his fiction "Telemachus" was interpreted by his friends and enemies as a satire against the extravagant rule of Louis XIV, who full of anger, made of Fénelon a sort of political prisoner in his diocese. The once popular archbishop worked among his people with humility, kindness and charity, hoping for a better day. His only hope for vindication and victory was pinned on the succession to the throne of his famous pupil, the duke of Burgundy. But this very hope came to nought, by the premature death of the young prince. Fénelon died in 1715, full of consciousness of his innocence, and firm in his religious convictions.

Fénelon's connection with the Jansenists and with the movement of Quiétisme perhaps needs further elucidation and account. The Jansenists represented a community of religious brothers, who, in opposition to the order of Jesuits, favored a more practical piety. Here we are not concerned with the doctrine of Grace over which they carried on a heated controversy with their opponents. That which interests us the most is "the little schools" of Port Royal which they conducted for the education of the young. These little schools of Port Royal were founded during the abbacy of Abbé Saint Cyran, in the rue Saint Dominique, at Paris. These schools had a very short-lived existence, from 1637-1661. They were shut down by the order of Louis XIV, through the instigation of the Jesuits. In spite of their short duration, they exercised important influences upon French education. These influences were due to the very spirit prevailing in these schools, which was love, and not severe discipline. The founder of these schools, Abbé Saint Cyran writes in a letter, "I wish you could read in my heart the affection which I have for children." Again, they were due to the profound faith in the urgency of education and the unflinching obligation of the parents for the education of their offspring. The Abbé Saint Cyran expresses this faith in the following statement: "as they hasten to baptism, so they should hasten to education and all that they do without education merely draws down God's curse on the father and mother, who are the visible guardian angels."[1] The little

---

[1] Cf. **Lettres Chrétiennes et Spirituelles** de Saint Cyran.

schools of Port Royal also introduced new and better methods of teaching than those which prevailed at that time. For instance, they taught reading through phonic method. They emphasized the teaching of the vernacular. In the University of Paris and in The Ratio Studiorum of the Jesuits, the vernacular was not given a place at this time. This was a salutary innovation. They prepared good text-books on grammar, philosophy and other school subjects.

A number of the great men of France have been connected with these little schools of Port Royal. Racine, the great tragedian, was their product. Pascal wrote his famous "Lettres Provinciales" in defense of the Jansenist movement. Such great teachers as Lancelot, Nicole, Guyot and Coustel were among the luminaries of these little schools. Jacqueline Pascal, sister of Blaise Pascal, who had charge of girls' education, is the author of "Réglements pour les Enfants de Port Royal," and an ardent worker for feminine education in France. Her plans, however, advocated a very strict ascetic way of education. In spite of a newer spirit in the little schools of Port Royal, the religion of this community was extremely austere and ascetic. Paroz, the author of the "Histoire Universelle de La Pédagogie," aptly evaluates the Port Royal schools, saying "If

France had developed the pedagogic work commenced by Port Royal it would be further advanced by almost two centuries."

Fénelon in his early years had leanings toward the Jansenist movements. By temperament and by his mysticism he belonged to that school.

His connection with "Quiétisme" again was the result of his mystic nature whose sole motive was love. Molinos, a Spanish Jesuit, taught that the soul, submerged in perfect contemplation of God, attains a state of calmness, or quietude. Hence "Quiétisme" meant the pure love of God, contemplation, a sort of passive ecstasy. This doctrine of Molinos was condemned at Rome in 1687. But a young widow, Mme Guyon, introduced "Quiétisme" in France. Mme de Maintenon and Fénelon adhered to it. At one time, it was introduced within the walls of Saint Cyr, girls' seminary, established by Mme de Maintenon and subsidized by Louis XIV; Bossuet, full of reason and logic, observed the inroads of "Quiétisme" in France and tried to check it. After a long controversy, he induced Fénelon and Mme Guyon to sign a formulary, indicting the extreme tenets of "Quiétisme." Not satisfied with this, Bossuet wrote his famous "Instructions sur les Etats d'Oraison," 1697. He submitted this to Fénelon for approval, but the latter hastened to publish his "Maximes des Saints," in defense of "Quiétisme." Bossuet through winning the influence of the court succeeded in having Fénelon's work condemned at Rome. Fénelon with apparent humility accepted defeat; however, he firmly believed in his own innocence.

Fénelon has exercised his influence on Mme de Maintenon, who organized the famous school of Saint Cyr, financed by the court of Louis XIV, for the education of young ladies not destined for the veil. Her school became famous, where young girls were given a more secular training, especially during the first period in the life of this institution, in pleasant atmosphere, with plays, games, and innocent enjoyment. Mme de Maintenon, haunted with the fear lest her pupils would turn précieuses,[1] restricted her curriculum. All ancient history was left out of it; very little modern history; enough general history. Geography was excluded as well as composition. Very little writing and spelling was permitted. She emphasized in this school gaiety, activity, simplicity, genuineness,—things that were lacking in the schools for women in their training, in convents. Racine wrote his religious tragedy espe-

---

[1] Cf. **Les Précieuses Ridicules** of Molière describes with mirth and pleasantry the utter artificiality of the 17th century young ladies.

cially for the school of Mme de Maintenon, who had ordered the great tragedian to "write, in his leisure moments, a kind of moral or historical poem, in which love is entirely left out." Racine wrote "Esther" in order " to be recited and sung." This was presented by the students of Saint Cyr, with a splendid success, according to the testimony of Mme de Sévigné, Mme de La Fayette and Mme de Caylus. Presentation of tragedies by the students of Saint Cyr was a step further in the education of girls in France. However Mme de Maintenon became more grave toward the end of her career and this, in its turn, had its reflection in the atmosphere of Saint Cyr.

After portraying the setting in which Fénelon, the artist teacher acted, it is fitting to enter now, in full detail, into the discussion of his more specific pedagogical contributions.

The educational theories of Fénelon are condensed chiefly in a charming book written with a facile, exquisite, clear pen, entitled "De l'Education des Filles," treatise on "The Education of Girls." This was written at the special request of the Duke and Duchesse de Beauvilliers, who had eight girls. As such, the book is dedicated to the education of the girls of nobility. But fortunately it is not limited to the narrow scope for which it was composed; it embraces the entire field of education. Especially chapters three to six deal with general principles of education, the remaining chapters being devoted more directly to the problem of girls' education. Fénelon, in this charming book, lays before the public, certain advanced educational ideas, long before the time of Rousseau, Pestalozzi and Froebel. Let us promptly enter into the analysis of these new ideas—new, viewed not from our present-day educational level of attainment but in the light of the educational thought and practice prevailing in his day.

Paul Janet laying before us the true picture of the status of feminine education at that time, points out the fact that Fénelon represents advanced thought in his work. According to Abbé Fleury, the education of women was generally accepted to be confined in the knowledge of "catechism, sewing, diverse little pieces of work, singing, dancing, making polite bows and speaking clearly."[1]

There were a few extremists who rebelled against this general view of feminine education. For instance, fourteen years before Fénelon wrote his treatise, Poilain de La Barre, a Protestant writer had published his treatise, "De l'Egalite des Sexes" (the Equality of the Sexes) in which he proclaimed:

---

[1] Cf. Fénelon, Paul Janet, p. 19.

"If the people would find it pleasant to see a woman teach eloquence and medicine, or act as a policeman, plead before judges as a lawyer, or act as a judge and render justice or lead an army, etc., it is because of lack of custom, and she will do it.[1]

Commenting on the contributions of Fénelon, Paul Janet makes the following fitting remark:

"The principle that dominates Fénelon's book is that of the dignity of woman, hence the need of instructing her and elevating her mind. Nothing is so progressive (liberal) as such a thought, nothing more conforming to what the future would proclaim for women."[2]

Again:

"This program besides those of present-day would seem perhaps a little modest and a little short, but, more than in his conclusions, we are interested in the spirit itself that inspires them. This spirit is eminently liberal, progressive. Fénelon long before Rousseau demanded that nature should be taken into account, that children should not be imposed upon by a material discipline which would nullify their activity and would cause their age to rebel. He has sensed the charm of childhood and has loved children. It is for this reason that he is a great educator and one of the masters of French pedagogy."[3]

A fine British author in evaluating the work of Fénelon reaches a similar conclusion: "Indeed, as one reads his book, one wonders sometimes why the two later writers," referring to Rousseau and Pestalozzi, "should have been praised as pioneers, may one say so inordinately? As observant as Pestalozzi, so much more reasonable

---

[1] Cf. Fénelon, Jaul Janet, p. 20.
[2] Cf. Ibid.
[3] Cf. Ibid.

than Rousseau, the Abbé de Fénelon has scarcely received the credit due to him."[1]

After a careful reading of his treatise on "The Education of Girls"[2] the impartial observer cannot help gleaning out the following educational principles which Fénelon proclaimed to the world.

I. **The Need of Education for Women.**—Fénelon through his practical experience gained at the institution, Des Nouvelles Catholiques, came to believe in the dignity of womanhood. Hence, he became an ardent pleader in favor of feminine education. In this belief and position he was far more advanced than most of his contemporaries. He was conspicuously more advanced than the famous writer and educational prophet, Rousseau, who successfully brought the claims of modern progressive education to the ears of his contemporaries. In this regard Fénelon writes:

"Nothing is more neglected than the education of girls. Custom and maternal caprice decides altogether everything in this matter: people suppose that little edu-

---
[1] Cf. Studies in French Education, p. 117.

[2] "I wish that anyone could show me a work beginning with the **Economics** of Xenophon up to the **Letters and Conversations** of Mme de Maintenon, which are after all inspired by Fénelon, a work in which shine an exact and true knowledge, a profound and penetrating experience of the heart. . . here is a book good for the girls of the nobility, of the bourgeoisie, of the common people, also useful for the adolescent youth of the masculine sex, a book good for all epochs . . ." XVIIe Siècle, Études Littéraires, E. Faguet, p. 355.

cation need be given to this sex. . . it is true that one must fear of making them ridiculous savants.[1] Women as usual have weaker minds and they are more curious than men—but what follows from the natural weakness of women? The weaker they are, the more important it is to strengthen them. Have they not duties to fulfill, duties which constitute the foundation of all human life." (Chapter I).

II. Developing Judgment and Personality.—

Like Montaigne he is an advocate of the training of judgment instead of stuffing the memory with useless bits of information. "Avoid from loading his memory: because it confuses and lies heavily on the brain; do not tire him with annoying rules and paradigms. . ." (Chapter V); again, "people make a dangerous impression of weariness (ennui) and sadness upon their temper by talking to them always about words and things which they do not understand at all; no freedom, no enjoyment, always lesson, silence, constrained posture, correction and threats." (Chapter V). Does not this sound like Rousseau or Dewey condemning verbal, formal education and stiff extraneous discipline? Fénelon encourages the questions of children: "As they are ignorant of many things, they have many questions to ask; so they ask many. It is sufficient to answer them precisely and add at times a few little comparisons so that they may better comprehend the

---
[1] Cf. Les Femmes Savantes, Molière, satirizes sophisticated women.

clarifications made to them. If they pass a judgment on something without knowing it well, embarrass them with a few new questions to make them realize their error without confusing them rudely." (Chapter V).

III. **Learning as Pleasurable Experience.**—Throughout his work Fénelon advocates a type of education which takes place in and through pleasurable experiences of the child. He condemns dogmatic, authoritarian education. Perhaps in his advocacy of making the learning process pleasurable he does not deeply comprehend the effectiveness of an intrinsically motivated learning act, rather, he advocates sugar-coating. In this regard, Rousseau far excells his predecessor, since he condemns clearly the teaching of reading through dices and games. Fénelon says: "I have seen various children who have learned while playing. One needs only to tell them things of joy and amusement which one takes out of a book in their presence, and unconsciously causing them to learn the alphabet. After this, they would wish on their own account to be able to go to the source which has caused them pleasure." (Chapter V.)

Condemning the austere and ascetic type of education he goes on saying: "Notice one of the great faults of ordinary educations. They lay all pleasure on one side and all weariness to the other; all weariness in studies, all pleasure in amusements. What can a child do except enduring impatiently this rule, and then running ardently after plays and games?" (Chapter V).

IV. Use of Right Motivation.—To motivate a child to act and to learn is the main function of a teacher. Fénelon, through keen observation, has learned the need of right motivation in order to make a child desire to learn. Teachers of composition may well study the following advice: "If you desire him to write something, tell him: 'write me a letter; send this or that thing to your brother or to your cousin.' All this pleases the child." (Chapter V). Emphasizing the educative value of praise, Fénelon says: "Although praises are to be feared because they may cause vanity, one must try to take advantage of them in order to encourage children, without intoxicating them." (Chapter V). The child must understand before he learns anything. He must be given a reason or he must see the aim in his learning activity. Fénelon dwelling on this thought, writes: "One must always show them a solid and agreeable purpose, to keep them steady in their work. One must never try to subject them to a dry and absolute authority." (Chapter V).

V. Emphasis on Physical Education.— Ancient Greeks as well as educators of the Renaissance laid a great stress on physical development. Medieval education, on the other hand, emphasized mortifying the flesh in order to strengthen the soul. Fénelon, an admirer of Hellenic culture, follows Plato's advice "gymnastic for the body, music for the soul." He says: "The most useful thing during the first years of infancy is to take care of the health of the child, to try to make his blood sweet by the proper choice of foods and by a simple regime of life, to regulate his meals so that he would eat always on the same hour and eat very often in proportion to his needs, and not eat outside of his meal hour." Chapter III). . . "Let a child play and mix instruction with play. . Avoid fatiguing him by an indiscrete exactness (exactitude)."

VI. Acute Observations of Human Nature— As all the educational theorists have drawn their thoughts from their observation of human nature, so Fénelon has been an excellent student of human nature and has given us some very excellent suggestions. In teaching, he points out the importance of proper distribution of time and the necessity of short periods of rest at intervals. Again, he stresses the need of early training of habits: "In order to remedy all these evils, it is very advantageous to start the education of girls from their very tender infancy. The first year during which the child is left to the care of indiscreet and at times intemperate women, however, is one in which the most profound impressions are made, and consequently it has a very great relation to the rest of her life." (Chapter III). Then he tells us about the influence of milder emotions on a child's learning and behavior: "simple pleasures are less intense and less vivid, it is true. The others carry away the soul by stirring the springs of passions. But the simple pleasures are of better use; they give an equable and durable joy without any bad results." (Chapter V). He also gives us a good advice on the psychology of approval and disapproval: "Do not tell a child his defect without adding a means of surmounting it, a means which will encourage him to do." Here is another sensible suggestion indicating an effective way of reconditioning a feeling of inferiority complex. After pointing out the connection of jealousy to inferiority, he says: "Give her from time to time little victories over those of whom she is jealous: induce her, if you can, to laugh with you freely at her timidity; show her some timid people who have at last conquered their temper; teach her at times by indirect ways that timidity and laziness strangle the mind." (Chapter V). He has indicated several other applications of psychology to the bringing up of the child but space does not permit us to make further quotations. True, he does not have the true science of psychology, especially in matters pertaining to the description of brain and its physiology, but who had correct ideas on the human brain before comparatively more recent times?

VII. Follow Nature.— Long before Rousseau, he reacted against the utterly artificial type of education and gave advice to study and to follow nature. "One must be content in following and aiding nature" (Chapted III). In his advocacy of natural education he is not an extremist. We know that he indulges in punishment at proper and psychological moments. His very character would have revolted against an inordinate worship of nature such as Rousseau had; he was a man of moderation, with Greek sense of proportion, in all things.

VIII. A Fine Method of Moral Education.— Fénelon throughout his writings advocates the effectiveness of moral education through indirection and suggestions. He does not advise to press matters with children. "A person might ask in their presence to another: 'Why are you doing this?' and the other would answer, 'I am doing it for this or that reason.' 'Why have you confessed your fault?' 'It is because I would commit a greater fault if I cowardly should tell a lie, and there is nothing more beautiful than frankly saying: I am wrong.' This whole thing must be done without any affectation." The third chapter of "The Girls' Education" is entirely devoted to the theme of imitation and the necessity of setting good examples before children. Here and there he emphasizes and re-emphasizes this point. "Do not fear of speaking the defects which are visible in you—tell her that by correcting your own defects you are setting an example for her to correct her own." (Chapter V). In the matter of punishment, Fénelon advocates that of natural consequences and he pleads for persuasion rather than imposition. "Without any extreme necessity do not take an austere and imperious air which makes children tremble. . . you would cause them to shut off their hearts and lose their confidence in you, without which no good fruit can be expected from education. Have yourself loved by them; let them feel free with you; let them not fear at all allowing their faults seen by you."

IX. Use of Stories in Character Formation.—Chapter VI is entirely devoted to the discussion of the importance of stories in the formation of character. "Children love with a passion ridiculous stories. . . Do not fail to take advantage of this inclination; select some animal stories which are ingenious and innocent in meaning. Tell them the story of Joseph. The child will be charmed in telling these stories." And he points out the use of dramatization: "If you have many children, get them used gradually to dramatize and present historical personages which they have learned."

Fénelon believed so much in the efficacy of stories and fables in character education that he himself wrote a book of "Fables" for his pupil, the duke of Burgundy. These fables compared to those of La Fontaine are not of very great literary value, nevertheless they are very instructive.

Besides fables, he wrote a book of dialogues, "Dialogues des Morts," in which through indirect suggestions his pupil found moral lessons: for instance, a lesson on war, given to the prince indirectly through this dialogue: "War is an evil which dishonors the human race. . . all wars are civil wars; since always they involve men against men." Here is another moral lesson given through indirection: "He who governs must obey the law the most." . . "It is not a man who must reign, but laws." . "Absolute power, far from assuring tranquility and authority to the princes, makes them unhappy and brings on their ruin."

Fénelon wrote also a pedagogical fiction, "Télémaque," which in addition to its literary charms, is a book of character training. It was written especially for the education of his princely pupil. In "Telemachus," Fénelon summarizes Greek history and mythology with an admixture of his own political and moral views. He writes as if he imagines he were continuing the fourth book of the Odyssey, in which young Telemachus sets out in search of his father, Ulyssus. But Fénelon makes him visit Phoenicia, Egypt, Cyprus, Crete, Hell, and the Island of Calypso. The moral lessons given to the Duke of Burgundy made it appear as though "Telemachus" was written as a satire against the great monarch, Louis XIV. Fénelon thereby lost the favors of the king and lived as a recluse in his diocese, deprived of his former influence and prestige. "Telemachus" is translated in almost every language, and it has been used in the past as a text-book of French in foreign countries.

X. Object Lessons and Experiencing.—Long before Rousseau and Pestalozzi Fénelon pointed out the importance of first hand observation of objects and learning through direct experiencing.

"The curiosity of children is an inclination which precedes instruction; do not fail in taking advantage of it. For example, in the fields, they see a mill, and they wish to know what it is, it is necessary to show them how this food that nourishes men is prepared. They see harvesters, it is necessary to explain to them what they are doing, how they sow the grain, and how these get multiplied in the soil. In the city they see shops where many arts are practiced, and where different sorts of merchandise are sold. Never must one be tired of their questions and requests; these are the avenues which nature offers you to facilitate your instruction. Show that you are pleased with them; through them you will imperceptibly teach them how the things that serve men are made, and on which business is revolved. Little by little, without any special study they will learn the good method of making all these things for their own use, and the exact price of each, which is the real foundation of economy. These informations should not be scorned by any person, since people need to avoid being cheated in their expenses, but these are especially necessary for girls to know." (Chapter II).

XI. Observations on Girls Defects.— In Chapters IX and X Fénelon writes down his observations on the defects of girls. No doubt they represent the defects of girls of his own race and of his own particular time. As conditions change and time advances, these defects change also. For instance, he points out the softness and timidity which characterize the training of girls of his own time. The modern program of physical education for girls in our schools coupled with all kinds of outdoor activities have changed the character of our modern girls in this respect. He advises to repress in girls exceedingly tender friendships, little jealousies, extravagant compliments and flatteries. He advises to teach them to say much in a few words. He indicates that the majority of women say little in many words. He complains of trickiness, pretension and false modesty, vanity, etc. He points out a way to cure them of these defects: "Try to make girls understand how honor that proceeds from a good conduct and from a real capacity is more estimable than that which comes from one's hair or one's clothes." Then he goes on discussing the duties of women. "She does not know the importance and the extent of things with which I propose to instruct her. . . what a discernment she needs in order to know the nature and the genius of each of her children, in order to find the most proper way of conducting herself with them and to discover their moods, their propensities, their talents, to prevent their budding passions, to teach them good maxims and to cure them of their faults! What a prudence does she need in order to acquire and conserve on them her authority without losing their friendship and confidence! But does not she need to observe and to know profoundly the people whom she places near them?" In chapter XII Fénelon discusses the art of employing domestics. "She must know how to manage them efficiently, with kindness, patience and tolerance."

Then, he describes the nature of the subject-matter and **The Curriculum** for the education of women.

Of course, he mentions reading, writing and arithmetic to begin with. Besides, they must learn the rudiments of law to be able to manage their estates. They may read the works of pagan authors, Greek, Roman and French history. He cautions the French girls from learning Italian and Spanish, lest they might read dangerous books. Instead, he advocates the study of Latin, "because that is the language of the church." With selection and discrimination they may read works of eloquence and poetry. But he cautions them against too much cultivating their imagination. Music and painting fall in the same category. Great care must be taken not to fall into the temptation of softening the mind. He says that a Christian music and poetry would be better.

In chapter XIII he discusses the problem of employing governesses and makes a few observations, full of common sense.

In his advice to a lady of quality he reiterates some of his pedagogical ideas. He agrees that the young lady would be better educated in her home under the supervision of her mother than if she were cloistered in a convent. But great care must be exercised in the selection of the servants. Then he makes the following remark which brings out the characteristic bent of his mind: "Have her understand that men are not made to be served." Again, "Masters who are better educated than their servants, being full of faults, must not expect that servants would be free from faults, since they have lacked instruction and good examples."

Fénelon's Success as a Tutor.—Besides the experience which Fénelon gained in Des Nouvelles Catholiques, he actually tutored three sons of the Grand Dauphin, the Duke of Anjou (who became king of Spain), the Duke of Berry, and chief among all, the Duke of Burgundy, who was to succeed Louis XIV to the throne. According to the testimony of Saint Simon, "the young duke was born terrible, headstrong and full of anger in the extreme, impetuous with fury, obstinate in the utmost—naturally inclined to cruelty, barbarous in raillery. . ." Fénelon, through the use of his pedagogical methods, and through his understanding, sympathy, kindness, tact and firmness succeeded eminently in training the young prince to be a well-behaved person. According to Des Granges "he succeeded too much, perhaps, because the Duke of Burgundy, when he became a man, was somewhat hesitating and timid. But he was loyal, conscious of his duties, and if a premature sickness had not taken him away from the hopes of the nation, he would at least have spared us the deplorable reign of Louis XV."[1]

That the personality of the teacher played an important part in the successful training of the unmanageable prince is borne out by the following anecdote related by Paul Janet in his book on Fénelon. One day Fénelon severely reproached the young prince. The young man rebelled and armed with his dignity and nobility of birth replied to his teacher: "No, sir, I know who I am and who you are." Fénelon did not answer him and did not say a word, and appeared profoundly sad. The next morning Fénelon presenting himself to the Duke of Burgundy, replying to the haughty offense of the preceding day, he said to him: "I am not afraid to tell you that I am above you. It is not a question of birth in this matter. You, no doubt, should know that I am above you on account of my wisdom and knowledge; you know only what I taught you, and that is nothing compared to what I can teach you. As for authority, you have none on me, and I, on the

---

[1] Cf. **Histoire de La Littérature Française**, Ch. M. Granges, p. 542.

other hand, have full and complete authority on you. You perhaps believe that I consider myself very happy for being provided with this work which I have with you. Undeceive yourself, sir, for I took this duty upon me only to obey the king; and so that you will not have any more doubt about this, I will take you to His Majesty to beg of him to appoint another one in my place whose cares may be more successful than mine, I hope." The Duke of Burgundy was very much terrified by this declaration. He wept and begged. Fénelon put off his decision to another day in order to have time for thinking, and seemed to yield only to the insistence of Mme de Maintenon.

This little incident shows how tactfully Fénelon managed the sophisticated and impetuous duke. No doubt, Fénelon possessed all the qualities that make a successful teacher. Consequently his educational theories are not the result of a fiery imagination but the product of an observing, penetrating, loving, affable, tactful, masterful artist-teacher. He not only is one of the founders of feminine education in France, but a worthy contributor to the general field of education throughout the world. It may seem strange that he is not commonly given his due place among the rank and file of educational theorists in the historical literature of American education. Yet he deserves such a recognition, to be sure, belated though it may be.

CHAPTER IV

Jean-Jacques Rousseau[1]

1712 - 1778

Rousseau, the Genevese simple Frenchman, whose passionate rhetoric inflamed the imagination of suffering mankind into possibilities of rightful living, whose powerful pen preached doctrines, political, social, artistic and educational, which revolutionized the whole realm of intellectual and social life of mankind, was the most peculiar of all men. As a writer he depicted the charms of a quiet, serene life, in the bosom of nature, in voluptuous enjoyment of the beauties of natural life, yet, far from enjoying tranquilly such a quiet life, he wandered from village to hamlet, from city to metropolis, from his native country to foreign countries; his life full of tortuous digressions, his mind subject to the mightiest of storms and his heart enslaved to the most degrading of passions. (This was Rousseau, a very consistent embodiment of inconsistencies.) He was the most ardent preacher of paternal affec-

---

[1]. This paper was read before a seminar group of graduate students in the History and Philosophy of Education, in charge of Dr. Lester B. Rogers, Dean of The School of Education, University of Southern California and then it was published in **Education**, vol. XLVIII, (1927) no. 2-3. With ample additions and revisions we are reprinting it here.

tion and parental responsibility for the rearing of offspring, yet in reality he proved to be one of the greatest of shirkers of all fathers; for he surrendered his own children to the care of a foundling asylum. He was one of the best painters of a virtuous domestic life, depicted in the pages of "La Nouvelle Héloise," where virtue and duty would reign supreme, while in actual practice he transgressed all the dictates of virtue and duty. It is therefore a futile task to try to discover consistency in Rousseau's life, not even in his writings. A modern psychologist would qualify him on the emotional side as a man of "artistic temperament," whose life was ugly but whose influence was great. And on the intellectual side he would be described as a very rare specimen of a man possessing an intuitive genius.

It was due to this anomalous character of Rousseau's nature that almost all the critics are bewildered before the task of evaluating him, as well as his work. Even Davidson, who at times scathingly and sometimes unjustifiably censures Rousseau in some respects and especially lays great stress on "his sensuous, indolent, dalliant nature" and characterizes his philosophy of life as a philosophy of "bovine" existence, even this same critic cannot help but admire Rousseau for his tremendously great influence "as the father of modern pedagogy," "father of modern democracy," and "political science," father of romanticism in literature, and naturalism in religion.

"That the influence of Rousseau's ideas upon educational theory and practice was, and is, great, no one will deny. In education, as in other things, his passionate rhetoric and his scorn for the conventional existent with the ideal simplicity of nature, roused men from their slumbers and made them reconsider all that they had so long blindly taken for granted and bowed before. And in so far, his work was invaluable. His bitter, sneering condemnation of the corrupt, hypocritical, fashionable life of his time, with the distorting, debasing, and dehumanizing notions of education and his eloquent plea for a return to life truly and simply human, and to an education based upon the principles of human nature and calculated to prepare for such a life, were righteous and well-timed. His purpose was thoroughly right and he knew how to make himself heard in giving expression to it. But when he came to inform the world in detail how this purpose was to be carried out, he undertook a task for which he was not fitted either by natural endowment or by education."[1]

Divergent Views on Rousseau.—In this connection it must be mentioned too, that there are also a few critics who are prone to belittle Rousseau's influence, because his work is full of contradictions and utopian chimeras. They characterize his work for lack of organization. They emphasize the fact that Rousseau did not possess an organically systematized knowledge, owing to his lack of methodic training. They also censure

---
[1] Cf. **Rousseau and Education According to Nature**, p. 212, Thomas Davidson.

him for his excessively weak sentimentality. They try to reduce his influence to a negligible quantity because his political and educational writings are not products of a reasoned-out meditation. They also do not forget to emphasize the fact that he drew his chief inspiration from Hobbes for his political doctrines and is indebted to Locke and Montaigne for his educational theories.

There is no doubt that some of these criticisms can be justified in some respects. But one essential factor must not be forgotten—namely, that Rousseau did not write his "Social Contract" or "Emile" in a period of quiet tranquility in the history of mankind. His own stormy life, the turbulent manifestations of unrest in the society of the eighteenth century in which he lived, and in addition to this, his own artistic temperament did not permit him to theorize serenely in the mood of a calm philosopher. On the contrary, in view of the horrible social maladies, he was shaken to the bottom of his heart and with all the vehemence of his passionate rhetoric he sounded the clarion call of rebellion against the existing wrong practices. His role, therefore, was that of a revolutionary who became a prophet to wake up mankind from its lethargy in order to break the chains of intellectual, social and ecclesiastical slavery, to emancipate humanity from the shackles of absolutism in politics, in thought, in religion, and to free childhood from the stifling oppression of lifeless tradition and routine.

Important Considerations in Judging Rousseau.—To judge Rousseau, to evaluate his work, one must first of all consider the historical setting in which the drama of modernization took place, Rousseau being one of the chief actors. "It is necessary to put aside all of one's prejudices against the weak and offensive personality of the author and to view the contradictions of his life and writings in their true perspective. His work on education is probably the most extraordinary union of strength and weakness, fascination and repulsion, high ideals and unpracticality, that was ever produced. But its errors and illusions are fully outweighed by great truths and lofty sentiments, and in making an appraisal, one should offset the grave defects of the book by its still larger merits."[1]

Rousseau's "Emile," with which we are concerned in this chapter more than with any other writings of his, is, and will remain forever, an epoch-making work, in spite of all contradictions that one may find in it alongside with the greatest of educational truths. Goethe aptly emphasized

---
[1] Cf. **Great Educators of Three Centuries**, p. 98, Frank P. Graves.

this point by a figure of speech, characterizing "Emile" as "the teacher's gospel."

Three Fundamental Errors in "Emile."—Indeed there are three fundamental and grave errors in "Emile" which must be clearly pointed out, and aside from these, one might read "Emile" as a modern treatise on pedagogy—a science which owes its rapid development to the publication of this much abused book. The three facts which Rousseau overlooked are as follows: (a) He did not realize that human nature is not exclusively individualistic but inherently social, hence society does not owe its existence to an artificially-drafted social contract but to the native sociability of the human soul. (b) Rousseau did not comprehend the fact that education does not and cannot take place in a social vacuum. (c) He utterly overlooked this other fact that education is capable of exercising its far-reaching influence upon the improvement of the social medium in which the individual is to be educated and socialized.

The Historical Setting.—Another important consideration in the evaluation of Rousseau's influence must not be lost sight of—namely, although most of his doctrines nowadays have been translated into ordinary and commonplace practices, they were the most novel and startling educational truths in his own day. To understand their revolutionary character, let us throw a fleeting glance into the educational thought and practice of his time.

Formalism, artificiality, empty rules of etiquette and courtliness were the supreme ideals of the educated class. Education was a privilege for the few. In France the most absolute monarchy reigned supreme, and surrounding the monarch there thrived a small coterie of courtly incense-burners. All social life and culture was centered in the court. The dancing-master was the educator of the day who did nothing but habituate young children to mimicry. Hence all education was memoriter and imitatory type of learning of the conventional rules and ways of dress, speech, manners, conduct and social intercourse. Not only in the court, but in all the princely mansions and salons the same artificiality and refinement was in vogue. The content of education, then, was not anything conducive to abundant learning and living; it was hollow, superficial, and nothing but artificial. Even Molière satirized this ridiculous tendency of artificiality in speech in his "Les Précieuses Ridicules."[1]

---

[1] Cf. **Les Précieuses Redicules,** Oeuvres Complètes de Molières, Oxford, à l'Imprimerie de l'Université, 1900, Londres.

The Child a Miniature Adult.—On the other hand the object of education, the child, was not held to be a young developing, growing, and unfolding soulful being, but rather a miniature adult, who was not permitted to indulge in a free, playful activity, or be occupied in spontaneous interests. Taine, in his "Ancient Regime," pictures the child life of the period in a very vivid and picturesque manner. "Little boys have their hair powdered, 'a pomatumed chignon, ringlets, and curls;' they wear the sword, the chapeau under the arm, a frill, and a coat with gilded cuffs; they kiss young ladies' hands with the air of little dandies. A lass of six years is bound up in a whalebone waist; her large hoop-petticoat supports a skirt covered with wreaths; she wears on her head a skilful combination of false curls, puffs, and knots, fastened with pins, and crowned with plumes, and so high that frequently 'the chin is half way down to her feet;' sometimes they put rouge on her face. She is a miniature lady and she knows it."[1]

Child's Nature and The Church.—While society regarded the child nothing but a miniature adult, the church did not consider him anything lofty. The nature of the child was considered de-

---
[1] Cf. **The Ancient Regime,** Taine, p. 137, Henry Holt & Company.

praved, sinful with original sin, and according to the then prevailing Calvinistic[1] point of view, children were the imps of Satan. Hence the function of education was to eradicate child's nature and to remake him into a perfect adult. Of course, it is very easy to visualize the agonies through which children had to go and the extraordinary repressive measures to which children were to be subjected. All education would be reduced to a slavish conformation on the part of every child to the austere models set by the ecclesiastical authorities. The method of education in such a scheme, naturally would be the catechetical repetitions of traditional knowledge, and subjection to very strict discipline, in which the free choice of the individual would have no place.

On the aesthetic side, the attitude of Calvinistic puritanism reflected itself in the content of education which was a negation of everything that was beautiful in nature and art. A somber, austere, dry and unattractive mass of information to be poured into the blank mind of the miniature adult, and a great number of supernatural fears to overwhelm the rebellious nature of the child's depraved heart.

Rousseau's Own Reaction.— Rousseau, born

---

[1] Even the Jansenists had the same view. Their zeal for the education of the young sprang from a desire to purge the depraved nature of the child.

and brought up in Geneva, was subjected to this kind of teaching as a child, when he was full of sentiment, emotion, imagination and life. His sentimental nature, guided by the flashing illumination of an intuitive genius, revolted against such practices, and he arose in solemn protest. As such, some of his doctrines were paradoxical, exaggerated, and one-sided, yet very valuable and necessary to bring about a desired change of attitude. A reasoned-out or logically-developed treatise on education would not and perhaps could not affect human thought so radically as did Rousseau's paradoxical, thought provoking, eloquent, and charmingly beautiful literary style which made an appeal to the heart of almost every reader, from the most sophisticated to the most simple and credulous one. His chief merit lies in the fact that he vitalized and popularized with his intuitive genius the thoughts and ideas which Hobbes, Locke or Montaigne conceived and preached. He was the supreme artist that inspired men in their innermost nature and thereby blazed a new and untrodden pathway in the minds of thinking people—the pathway of modern thought, in politics, philosophy, and education.

In the light of the then prevailing ideas of extreme artificiality and wrong conceptions of human nature as being basically depraved, was it not natural for Rousseau to shout his protest in an exaggerated and paradoxical manner? That "Tout est bien sortant des mains de l'Auteur des choses, tout dégénère entre les mains de l'homme."[1]

The Stronger the Persecution the Greater his Influence.—Is it not a sufficient proof in itself, attesting to the highly influential character of Rousseau's work, that the archbishop of Paris officially condemned "Emile" as soon as it was published, and the high dignitaries of the Church and State caused this book to be burned. Not only in Paris, but even in his native town his book was burned and the gates of Geneva were closed against him, so astounding were his protests, so startling were his revelations of truth, so advanced were his ideas, and so beyond the comprehension of his contemporaries were his theories! Nevertheless men of imagination, foresight and deep thinking grasped the essence of his thoughts in every land, particularly in Germany, France and Switzerland, and there resulted an immediate revolution in thought for a better understanding of human nature, human rights, children and their education. Paulsen relates that in Germany Rousseau's influence has been exceedingly great.

---

[1] This is the opening sentence of **Emile**: "Everything is good coming from the hands of the Creator of all things; everything degenerates in the hands of man."

Through Herder—Rousseau of Germany—Basedow and Salzmann, Rousseau's educational theories were put in practice, and their shortcomings were observed and their advantages were noted and improved upon. Kant, Fichte, Goethe, and Shiller became the admirers of Rousseau. Pestalozzi in Switzerland put in practice what Rousseau advocated in theory. Pestalozzi excelled Rousseau in two points: he utilized the social medium as an educative medium and emphasized the importance of education for the improvement of society. "The happiest educational results of Rousseau came through Pestalozzi. Rousseau had shattered the eighteenth century temple of despotism, privilege and hypocrisy, but it remained for Pestalozzi to erect a more enduring structure out of the ruins. It was Pestalozzi that developed the negative and inconsistent naturalism of "Emile" into a positive attempt to reform corrupt society by proper education and a new method of teaching."[1] Again "Pestalozzi's doctrines were neither very original, nor well carried out. His merit lay in making concrete and positive the abstract and general principles of Rousseau and in applying them to the schools."[2] Later on Herbart, Froebel, their disciples, and in modern times

---
[1] Cf. **Great Educators of Three Centuries,** Frank Graves, p. 122.
[2] Cf. Ibid., p. 149.

Colonel Parker and Dewey greatly improved on Rousseau's doctrines and caused their spirit to be incorporated in modern practice. This does not imply that they all derived their concepts from Rousseau, but there is no doubt that his inspiration and spirit permeated the entire educational field.

Biography of Rousseau.— Rousseau was born in Geneva, 1712. His mother died upon giving birth to him. The ancestors of Rousseau were French by origin and Protestant by faith. They had fled from France to avoid religious persecution and had secured the right of citizenship in the Calvinistic city of Geneva in 1550. Jean-Jacques' father, Isaac Rousseau, had a spirit of adventure; he had travelled in search of fortune; he had even tried to seek it in Constantinople, but failing this, he had returned to Geneva and settled at his work as watchmaker. His mother came from a line of Protestant pastors, Bernards. Jean-Jacques' mother, however, showed inclinations to frivolity. His older brother had disappeared one day never to be heard from again. Motherless young Jean-Jacques enjoyed only the inadequate guidance of his father, who himself was a very weak character. The education that the older Rousseau gave to this highly emotional and imaginative boy was extremely faulty. He encouraged

Jean-Jacques to read sentimental stories, sometimes even very late at night. The "Lives" of Plutarch was one among the best books that Jean-Jacques read and enjoyed. The young boy, at the age of ten, was left in charge of his uncle, Mr. Bernard, who left him at the home of a pastor, Mr. Lambercier. Jean-Jacques having spent two years here, came back to Geneva and worked as apprentice to an engraver. One night he was out very late. The gates of Geneva were closed. He fled to Confignon, a nearby Catholic village, rather than face punishment for his tardiness. A good-hearted priest sent him to Mme de Warens at Annecy. She was a zealous Catholic helping to convert young Protestants. In her turn, she sent him to a monastery at Turin, to catechize him in the doctrines of the Roman church. Jean-Jacques remained there only four months, and left the place as a Catholic. Then followed a period of precarious existence for Rousseau. He tried to make his living as a lackey; he went to Lyons accompanied by a musician; then to Geneva, Berne and Paris. Finally he made a journey on foot back to Mme de Warens at Annecy, then at Charmette, near Chambéry (1731). Rousseau led with Mme de Warens and her chaotic household "a pseudo-idyllic, kennelpoetic existence" as Dr. James Phinney Munroe[1] very aptly characterizes

---

[1] Cf. **Educational Ideal**, James Phinney Munroe, p. 156. D. C. Heath & co. Boston.

it. After Jean-Jacques abandoned this idyllic life, he became tutor (1740) to the children of the grand marshall of Lyons, M. de Mably. He made a failure as a tutor. Rousseau returned to Charmette once more, where he had learned to love nature and the beauties of the country. But soon he left Mme de Warens, this time once for all. Rousseau later came to Paris in 1741. There he was to be disappointed at first. He presented the new system of musical notation which he had invented, to the French Academy of Sciences, but he did not find any favor. However, thanks to the friendship of Mme Dupin, he obtained a secretarial position with M. de Montaigu, the French ambassador at Venice. But as usual he did not get along with his master. Then the young Rousseau returned to Paris, hoping to make a success as a musical composer. He wrote articles on music for the Encyclopedia of Diderot. Jean-Jacques composed the words as well as the music of an opera, "Les Muses Galantes," (1745). He cultivated the friendship of great and influential men, Fontenelle, Marivaux, Condillac and Voltaire. Through the advice of Diderot he took part in an essay contest proposed by the Academy of Dijon in 1749. The subject was "Whether the progress of sciences and of arts had contributed to pervert or to purify morals." Defending the negative side he won the prize. Thus, at once he became famous as the author of the "Discours sur des Sciences et les Arts" (1750) (Discourse on the Sciences and of Arts). He had a chance to obtain a pension from the court, but he did not care to have it. Money was of little import for Rousseau. He lived illicitly with Thérèse Levasseur, an uncultured peasant girl, who later became his wife. Of this marriage he had five children whom he abandoned to a foundling asylum. About 1754 he obtained again his right to citizenship of the Calvinistic city of Geneva by returning to the fold of the Protestant faith. He did not, however, dare to live in that city. The Academy of Dijon offered another literary contest in 1775 on the subject of "The Origin of the Inequality Among Men." Rousseau took part in it but did not receive the prize; however, the publication of his essay brought an unusual glory to him. Drunk with success and pride, he quarrelled with his friends. Therefore he was compelled to leave Paris. In 1756 he was offered by Mme d'Epinay a little cottage, the Ermitage, in the forest of Montmorency, near the castle of the Chevrette. He enjoyed in this beautiful spot peaceful tranquility for a short period. Here he started to write his two most important works, "Emile" and "The New Heloisa." But his peaceful life was not without its difficulties and bitterness. He had constant quarrels with his coarse wife and also with his friends; he fell in love with Mme d'Epinay's sister-in-law, Mme d' Houdetot. Under these circumstances he became a "persona non grata." Hence, he was compelled to leave the Ermitage (1757). He then settled in the village of Montmorency in a small house, where he lived tranquilly for a while. There he wrote his famous letter on "The Spectacles" by which he aroused the enmity of Voltaire. He finished "The New Heloisa" (1761), his "Social Contract," and "Emile" (1762). The parliament ordered "Emile" to be burned. To escape arrest Jean-Jacques slipped away quickly. He then wandered from city to city. Even Geneva, his birthplace, closed its gates against him. He went to several places, even to England where he was not able to live in harmony with his hospitable friend, Hume, the British philosopher. After wandering a while, Rousseau returned to Paris in 1770. While living in a small house, he wrote his "Confessions," and was again surrounded by his admirers. Yet he lived a very sickly and miserable life, suffering with delusions of persecution. M. de Girardin offered him the hospitality of his castle of Ermenonville. Rousseau, having lived there a few weeks only, died suddenly from an attack of apoplexy, in 1778, July 2.

Emile and The New Heloisa.—Among Rousseau's literary and philosophical works we are chiefly concerned with "Emile" and also to a slighter degree with the "New Heloisa." The latter is a romantic novel in which Rousseau exalted domestic virtue, with masterful descriptions of a simple life in the bosom of nature. In it there is a chapter[1] which deals with education. However, Rousseau amplified the contents of this chapter and incorporated it in his chief educational work, "Emile." This is composed of five books.

Books I and II treat the problems of Emile's education up to the age of twelve. Up to this age Emile must not receive any intellectual and moral education. Nature must take its own course. Nature being good, it must not be interferred with. This is the period when Emile's body and sense organs should be developed.

Book III takes the second period of Emile's education, from the age of twelve to fifteen. During this period Emile should receive his intellectual training. It is a relatively short period to master physical sciences, astronomy, geography and modern languages, which form the core of the curriculum advocated by Rousseau. He does not advise the teaching of history, grammar or ancient languages. Rousseau declares that he hates

---
[1]. Fifth Part, Third Letter.

books, "they teach us merely to speak of things we do not know." He recommends the Robinson Crusoe as the chief text-book for Emile. At the age of fifteen Emile learns a trade, as prescribed by Rousseau.

Book IV takes up the period from the age of fifteen to twenty. This is the period during which Emile is to receive moral and religious training. He is mature enough to understand moral and religious concepts. Rousseau is a theist believing in religious naturalism. The profession of Faith of the Vicar of Savoyard[1] expresses beautifully the religious concepts of Jean Jacques.

Book V is devoted to Sophie or the wife. Rousseau's concept of feminine education is very low. In this matter he could learn a great deal from Fénelon. He does not seem to have any high opinion of women. He says: "The wife is especially created to please the man."[2]

In analyzing his scheme of education, one is at once inclined to raise several questions; for instance, why divide four periods in Emile's life with a sharp line of demarcation, each with an exclusively distinct educational regime? Does not mental development of Emile start at a very

---

[1]Cf. **Emile,** Garnier Frères, p. 309.
[2]Cf. "La femme est specialement pour plaire a l' homme." **Emile,** Book V.

early age as it does with other children? Why postpone, then, the intellectual education to the ages twelve to fifteen? Again, does not Emile begin forming his moral character from the earliest childhood? Why postpone, then, his moral education to the age of fifteen to twenty? One can go on asking an infinite number of questions about the shortcomings of Rousseau's scheme as a systematic plan of education. His chief merit lies not in his scheme of education but in the flashes of new thoughts to which his genius gave a living form which he beautifully embodied in writing. Gleaning carefully from his works we shall endeavor to set forth some of these significant thoughts.

ROUSSEAU'S EDUCATIONAL IDEAS

I. Rousseau, the emancipator of childhood. —He was the first writer of importance who succeeded in making his voice heard for the emancipation of childhood from age-long prejudices, and from the oppressive trammels of medieval thought.

"Considering childhood all by itself is there in the world a being more weak, more wretched, more at the mercy of his surroundings, than a child who needs in such a great degree pity, love and protection? Does it not seem that it is for this reason that the first voices which are suggested to him by nature are cries and complaints?"[1] Again in "Emile" he pleads for children: "Do you tell me that the first sounds they make are cries? I can well believe it; you thwart them from the time they are born. The first gifts they receive from you are chains, the first treatment they undergo is torment. Having nothing but the voice, why should they not use it in complaints? . . O men, be humane! It is your highest duty; be humane to all conditions of men, to every age, to everything not alien to mankind. What higher wisdom is there for you than humanity? Love childhood; encourage its sports, its pleasures, its lovable instincts."

This fervently sentimental appeal of Rousseau was more than necessary to bring a change in the attitude of mankind toward childhood. In Rousseau's days the new-born children were bound up in swaddling clothes and their free movements and development were checked, even in the most advanced countries of Europe. The growing children, even in the palaces, were subjected to a process of withering, thanks to the strictly disciplinary and highly formal training they received. Even children and their mothers in princely man-

---

[1] Cf. The Third Part, Fifth Letter, of the **La Nouvelle Héloise**.

sions were not free to see each other as often as they would wish, and their most intimate relations were subjected to the most conventional, empty and repressive rules of etiquette. A modern Spanish playwright, Gregorio Martinez Sierra, in his drama entitled "El Palacio Triste"[1] (The Sad Palace), paints in a most gripping fashion the hollowness of such practices, from which the princess-mother and her children escape finally by fleeing away from the confines of the sad palace. It must be admitted, therefore, that Rousseau served humanity through the magic force of his eloquent rhetoric in bringing about a changed attitude of mind, favoring the free and untrammeled development of childhood.

II. Education as a Process of Living and not Merely Preparation.— Before the publication of "Emile" the paramount purpose of education was to prepare the miniature adult for a definite adult life, in the future. The entire period of childhood was considered a necessary evil, a waste of time, out of which the sooner the child would emerge the better. Rousseau saw the futility of this education, whose sole purpose was fixed in some distant future and he protested vehemently. "How to live is the business I wish to teach." Referring

---

[1]Cf. **El Palacio Triste,** Martinez Sierra, Ginn & Co.

to Emile, his pupil, he wrote: "On leaving my hands he will not, I admit, be a magistrate, a soldier, or a priest; first of all he will be a man." In his "Democracy and Education," does not Dewey rightly emphasize this truth by saying that education is not preparation for life, but it is life? And Rousseau preaches the gospel of a dynamic education in these words: "It is less important to keep him from dying than it is to teach him how to live. To live is not merely to breathe, it is to act; it is to make use of our organs, of our senses, of our faculties, of all the powers which bear witness to us of our own existence." Rousseau was right when he condemned the exclusively preparatory character of the current education. "Of all children born, only about half reach youth; it is probable that your pupil may never attain manhood. What, then, must be thought of that barbarous education which sacrifices the present to an uncertain future, and begins, by making him wretched, to prepare for him some far-away indefinite happiness he may never enjoy!"

III. The Nature of the Child the Starting Point for Education.—"Rousseau was a psychologist of the first rank."[1] His greatest contribution

---
[1] Cf. **Rousseau and Education According to Nature**, p. 107, Thomas Davidson.

to education lies in the fact that he has been the chiefest proponent of child study and child psychology. As we have seen before, his contemporaries did not trouble themselves at all to discover the nature of children, to study its characteristic tendencies, manifestations, laws, etc. It never occurred to them that each child had a mind of his own, and his life was governed by the activities of that particular mind. They were mostly concerned in suppressing the natural tendencies of that mind and supplanting it by an external mold. It was Rousseau who pointed out this error in the Preface of Emile: "We do not know childhood. Acting on the false ideas we have of it, the farther we go the farther we wander from the right path. Those who are wisest are attached to what is important for men to know, without considering what children are able to apprehend. They are always looking for the man in the child, without thinking of what he was before he became a man. This is the study upon which I am most intent, to the end that, though my method may be chimerical and false, profit may always be derived from my observations. I may have a very poor conception of what ought to be done, but I think I have a correct view of the subject on which we are to operate. Begin, then, by studying your pupils more thoroughly, for it is very certain that you do not know them."[1] It is a well-known fact that in this respect there prevailed a very deep ignorance and he aptly pointed out to his contemporaries the necessity of understanding the child. "Shall we never learn to put ourselves in the child's place? We do not enter into his thoughts, but suppose them exactly like our own."

In his study of child psychology Rousseau emphasized the importance of: (a) The individual differences existing among children. "Each has his own cast of mind, and in accordance to which he must be directed; and if we would succeed, he must be ruled according to this natural bent and no other. Be judicious, watch nature long, and observe your pupil carefully before you say a word to him. At first leave the germ of his character free to disclose itself."

(b) He recognized the stages of development in the child's growth and made known to the world that each of these stages has certain characteristic activities which must be given ample opportunity for expression. Although he drew a hard and fast line of demarcation, by dividing the period of growth into four distinct stages—from birth to five years of age, from five to twelve, from twelve to fifteen, and from fifteen to twenty—his obser-

---

[1] Cf. "Commencez donc par mieux étudier vos élèves, car très assurément vous ne les connaissez point." Préface, **Emile,** by Garnier Frères.

vation was not very far from our present-day knowledge of the psychology of growth. "Nature wants the children to be children before they become men. If we pervert this order, we shall produce precocious fruits, which will have neither maturity, nor taste, and soon will perish. We will have youthful doctors but old children."[1] And again in "Emile:" "Each age, each period of life, has its proper perfection, a sort of maturity which is all its own." In addition to this, he called attention to the period of adolescence and to the gradual awakening and waning of instinctive tendencies.

(c) Interest versus effort. Rousseau did not believe in an education which was to be imposed upon the child from without by external force and pressure. According to him one's education should grow out of his native interests. In this respect he was more modern in his psychological conception than the illustrious author of this often quoted saying: "Keep the faculty of effort alive in you by a little gratuitous exercise every day. That is, be systematically heroic in little unnecessary points, do every day or two something for no other reason than its difficulty.[2] Rousseau's

---

[1] Cf. **La Nouvelle Hèloise,** The Education of Children
[2] Cf. **Talks to Teachers on Psychology and to Students on Some of Life's Ideals,** by William James, p. 75; Henry Holt & Co., New York, 1913.

ideas on the question of interest were startlingly novel for the eighteenth century, when education was nothing but the complete subservience of the child to the iron rule of authority. Dewey would have been stoned for his doctrine of interest had he lived in Rousseau's time. In "Emile" he writes that "much attention is paid to finding out best methods of teaching children to read. . . A better thing than all these, a thing no one thinks of, is the desire to learn. Give the child this desire and you will not need dice or reading lotteries."

IV. Memoriter T y p e of Education Condemned.—Almost in every phase of contemporary education Rousseau finds an opportunity to condemn the educational practice of making children memorize everything they learn: poetry, philosophy, science, morals and religion. He rightly believes that the child can commit to memory with perfection anything that he is asked to learn; he may even recite it with a semblance of understanding; yet, in the true sense of the word, he never comprehends it for the simple reason that what he has learned has not been transformed into genuine thoughts or ideas through the exercise of his own thinking. In "The New Heloisa" Rousseau describes the more rational method of Julie's teaching her children, and he questions her regarding the teaching of the catechism. "Why do not your children learn (in the sense of memorizing) their catechism? 'In order that some day they may believe it,' said she. 'I want to make them Christians'." Since Rousseau's days educational practice has changed in this regard and we nowadays emphasize thinking rather than rote memory. "You cannot give ready-made ideas," says Dewey. (All we can do is to stimulate the thinking of children to think out their own problems.) We understand the uselessness of amassing isolated information and knowledge without relating them to one's experience and thinking. We believe that a man may be a walking encyclopedia, so far as lifeless knowledge is concerned, and yet he may be a man without power of thinking and acting. We owe a great debt to Rousseau for convincingly proving to his contemporaries the emptiness of the memoriter type of education.

V. Education by Direct Experiencing.—As a corrollary to the previous thought, Rousseau advocated that one's education will grow out of his experience rather than out of memorizing ready-made ideas of others. **The ancient Greeks had recognized the importance of doing in the educative process.** But during Rousseau's time people paid no attention to doing or experimental learning: acting, undergoing and testing the results. It was Rousseau who raised his voice in favor of this fundamental truth: "Do not give your pupil any sort of lesson verbally; he ought to receive none except from experience." And in another connection he repeated: "We should teach as much as possible by actions and say only what we cannot do."

As a consequence, the acceptance of Rousseau's theory naturally would result in a wholesale reversal of the formal and traditional method of verbal teaching. Thus the significance of experience as a factor in learning was emphasized by Rousseau most vehemently, but the educational world needed a profound and rational thinker like Dewey, to analyze this concept into its component parts and through logical thinking to draw up a sane philosophy of experience.

VI. The Importance of Physical Activities. —Rousseau pointed out the significance of physical activities in building up a vigorous, healthy body as well as a sound thinking mind. "If, then, you mean to cultivate your pupil's understanding, cultivate the strength it is intended to govern. Give him constant physical exercise, make his body sound and robust, that you may make him wise and reasonable. Let him be at work doing something; let him run, shout, be always in motion; let him be a man in vigor, and he will sooner become one in reason. . . To imagine that physical exercise injures mental operations is a wretched mistake; the two should move in unison and one ought to regulate the other." It is no wonder, that in every civilized country the physical activities of children, their plays and games no longer are frowned at by the grownups, due to the fact that the ideas of Rousseau and those of the subsequent educators have been steadily shaping our educational thought and practice.

VII. Training of the Senses and the Objective Teaching.—Rousseau advocated a many-sided education by which the pupil would be enabled to adjust himself to varying conditions in life. For such an ability one needed to train all of his senses, in their use and refinements. (He emphasized the importance of bringing the children in close contact with the objects by which they are surrounded.) In his view of sense perception and training of the senses he was more rational than his followers who in actual practice were satisfied by merely teaching observation, without any thinking process being involved in it and by describing the qualities of objects without actively making use of them.

"How far ahead he was of the psychology of his own day in his conception of the relation of the senses to knowledge! The current idea (and one that prevails too much even in our time) was that the senses were a sort of gateway and avenue through which impressions traveled and then built up knowledge pictures of the world. Rousseau saw that they are a part of the apparatus of action by which we adjust ourselves to our environment, and then instead of being passive receptacles they are directly connected with motor activities—with the use of hands and legs. In this respect he was more advanced than some of his successors who emphasized the importance of sense contact with objects, for latter thought of the senses simply as purveyors of information about objects instead of instruments of the necessary adjustments of human beings to the world around them."[1]

VII. Methods in the Teaching of Specific Subjects.— Rousseau applied his philosophy of teaching to various subjects in the schools. (a) Geography must be taught not merely from maps or books but from actual exploration, from close observation of home surroundings and gradually extending to the external world:

"When you are ready to teach the child geography, you get together your globes and your maps; and what machines they are! Instead of using all these representations, why do you not begin by showing him the object itself, so as to let him know what you are talking of? . . The two starting points in his geography should be the town in which he lives, and his father's house in the country. Afterward shall come the places lying between these two; then the neighboring rivers; lastly, the aspect of the sun, and the manner of finding out where the east is. This last is the point of union. Let him make himself a map of all these details, a very simple map. . . Be-

---

[1] Cf. **Schools of Tomorrow**, p. 12. John Dewey.

sides, the important thing is, not that he should know the exact topography of the country, **but that he should learn how to find out by himself."**[1]

(b) History: According to Rousseau's conception history should never be taught to very young children, especially as ready-made judgments about historical facts, and it should appear very late in the educational program. "The worst historians for a young man are those who judge. The facts, the facts; then let him judge for himself. If the author's judgment is forever guiding him, he is only seeing with the eye of another, and as soon as this eye fails him, he sees nothing."

(c) Languages: Rousseau, as a pupil studying Latin, was exasperated with all analytical, grammatical and symbolical teaching of languages. Therefore, he advocated the practical method of conversational teaching. "I would like the first articulate sounds he (Emile) must hear to be few in number, easy, distinct, often repeated. The words they form should represent only material objects, which can be shown him." Then he goes on in condemning our readiness "to content ourselves with words that have no meaning to us," and he points out that children "seem, at first, to have a grammar adapted to their own age," and he suggests to the teachers of language "always to speak correctly in their

---

[1] Cf. The emphasis is mine.

presence." Basedow, inspired by Rousseau, began to teach languages in Germany through conversational method, which gradually modified itself into what we now call the direct method.

(d) Sciences: In the teaching of sciences Rousseau advocated the need of teaching the pupils to become discoverers rather than imitators, and argued that the teacher of science should proceed through psychological rather than logical presentation of the subject matter. As Dewey rightly preaches, the first approach to subject matter should be as unscholastic as possible, so Rousseau emphasizes the same principle: "The thing is, not to teach him knowledge, but to give him a love for it, and a good method, acquiring it when this love has grown stronger. . . In investigating the laws of nature, always begin with the most common and most easily observed phenomena and accustom your pupil not to consider these phenomena as reasons, but as facts. . . I would not have my pupil study them in a laboratory of experimental physics. I dislike all the array of machines and instruments. The parade of science is fatal to science itself. . . I would make all our own machines, and not begin by making the instrument before the experiment has been tried. But after apparently lighting by chance on the experiment, I should by degrees invent instruments for verifying it."

(e) Nature study and art. Through Rousseau's exaltation of nature there came about a love for nature and an eagerness for a closer study of nature, which led to the development of natural sciences as well as a method of teaching them through field explorations and observations. Furthermore, people began to appreciate beauty of nature more and more and this new attitude resulted in the emphasis laid on the teaching of art and aesthetics.

IX. Industrial Education.— In Rousseau's time handwork was scorned. Aristocracy and nobility and all the people belonging to the upper classes enjoyed luxurious idleness. The purpose of education was not to fit the individual for useful occupations. Only common people needed to toil with their hands. And for this they did not need any education. It was Rousseau who for the first time trumpeted the rebellion against this fatal social conception, and with good reason he advocated that every individual should learn a trade: "To work is an indispensable duty in the social man. . ." Speaking about his pupil he said: "He must work like a peasant and think like a philosopher, or he will be as idle as a savage. . . Of all occupations fitted to yield man a subsistence, that which comes nearest to the state of nature is manual toil; of all conditions, the most independent of fortune and of man, is that of the artisan. He depends only on his labor; he is as free as the ploughman is bound; for the latter is tied to his land, whose crop is at the mercy of others." Rousseau recognized the importance of a useful occupation as a preparation against the vicissitudes of fate. His conception, however, did not go beyond the economical necessity and he did not conceive the psychological factor involved in the learning and practising of a useful handicraft. Nevertheless Pestalozzi, and especially Fellenberg and Froebel improved upon his ideas and as a result there came into existence movements of manual training, trade and industrial education.

Moral Training.— Rousseau, whose moral conduct was not exemplary by any means, advanced certain sane ideas for the teaching of morals. Of course, his abhorrence for all authority led him to an exaggerated attitude in this respect, but he indicated the fact that morals and religion cannot be taught through catechism; on the contrary they can be inculcated through example: "Remember, that before you venture undertaking to form a man, you must have made yourself a man; you must find in yourself the example you ought to offer him. . . Always preaching, always moralizing, always acting the pedant, you give them twenty worthless ideas when you think you are giving them one good one. Full of what is passing in your own mind, you do not see the effect you are producing upon others." (In respect to discipline, he advocated the punishment of natural consequences.) Although this method can be carried too far, even to defeat its own ends, nevertheless it does not cease from having something good in it. "He breaks the furniture he uses. Be in no hurry to give him any more; let him feel the disadvantages of doing without it. He breaks the windows in his room; let the wind blow on him night and day. Have no fear of his taking cold; he had better take cold than be a fool."

Rousseau has been very much criticized by some critics for his doctrine of moral training. But, from the vein of these criticisms one might detect that they were confusing Rousseau's personality with his ideas about morals and religion. It is admitted by great critics that his influence has been very good in favor of a devout conception of naturalistic religion. John Morley very aptly evaluates Rousseau's influence: "The most valuable of Rousseau's notions about education, though by no means consistently adhered to, was his urgent contempt for this fatuous substitution of spoken injunctions and prohibitions, for the deeper language of example, and the more living instruction of visible circumstance. The vast improvements that have since taken place in the theory and the art of education all over Europe and of which he has the honor of being the first and most widely influential promoter, may all be traced to the spread of this vast principle and its adoption in various forms."[1]

XI. Democratic Conceptions of Education. —Rousseau, the smasher of petrified notions prevailing about the superiority of aristocracy and their privileges, and the utter worthlessness of common people, did not, in his works, advocate the need of a universal and free education. But his political doctrine of liberty, equality, fraternity, once put in practice, would and did result in the establishment of a universal system of education. He was the father of democracy and his ideas inspired the outburst of the popular demand for equal rights, which culminated in the French revolution. "If the American revolution was due to the spirit of liberty inherent in the English people, the formulas in which the Declaration of Independence was couched were largely drawn from Rousseau. When its framers demanded

---
[1] Cf. Rousseau, p. 211, Vol. II, John Morley.

life, liberty, and the pursuit of happiness for every citizen, they were speaking in his language."[1] Rousseau's exaltation of the worth of the common people verges on the confines of a religious zeal: "It is the common people who compose the human race; what is not the people is hardly worth taking into account."

In concluding this paper, we feel justified in affirming that Rousseau has been the prime promoter of our modern educational thought and practice. It is true, he had some insane ideas; on the other hand he had many sane ones which would more than compensate and counterbalance the bad ones. We say that most of his advanced ideas (too advanced for his time) have been duly incorporated into our present-day educational system. Would that this were a fact! Is it not pertinent to ask ourselves if, even at the present time, we are not behind in putting into practice what we accept in theory to be sane and good? Are we in all circumstances basing our teaching on a foundation of doing and experiencing? Are we developing our subject matter on the basis of psychological rather than logical procedure? Are we proceeding in such a way that our pupils in science, history, geography, etc. are becoming dis-

---

[2]Cf. **Rousseau and Education According to Nature,** p. 233, Thomas Davidson.

coverers rather than imitators? Can we say that we are not teaching any longer to our pupils enclyclopedic chunks of information unrelated to thinking? Are we encouraging self-activity, development of initiative and genuine thinking in our pupils? One might prolong the series of these questions, but upon our positive answer will depend our consciousness of our progress in modern education, whose foremost precursor has been this ailing, imaginative, dreaming, and sentimental writer, Rousseau, one of the strangest persons of all the ages.

Rousseau has still some excellent ideas which will influence in time our educational thought and practice. His apotheosis of simple life and simple diet may guide us in our efforts to check the increasing artificiality and formalism prevalent in our social life.

BIBLIOGRAPHY

A Brief List of Books of General Character for a Back-Ground in Modern Educational Thought and Practice

Democracy and Education, John Dewey, MacMillan Co., New York, 1925.

Interest and Effort, John Dewey, Houghton Mifflin Co., 1913.

Schools of Tomorrow, John Dewey and Evelyn Dewey, E. P. Dutton & Co., New York, 1915.

Moral Principles in Education, John Dewey, Houghton Mifflin Co., New York, 1909.

Human Nature and Conduct, John Dewey, Henry Holt & Co., 1922.

The School and Society, University of Chicago Press, 1915.

Experience and Nature, Dewey, Open Court Publishing Co., Chicago, 1925.

Educational Frontiers, W. H. Kilpatrick and others, Century Co., New York, 1933.

Foundations of Method, W. H. Kilpatrick, The MacMillan Co., 1926.

Education For a Changing Civilization, W. H. Kilpatrick, The MacMillan Co., 1926.

Source Book in The Philosophy of Education, W. H. Kilpatrick, The MacMillan Co., 1924.

Outline of a Course in The Philosophy of Education, J. A. Macvannel, The MacMillan Co., 1912.

Living and Learning, Daniel Leary, Richard R. Smith Co., New York, 1931.

What is Education? by Ernest Carroll Moore, Ginn & Co., Boston, 1915.

Principles of Education, William Carl Ruediger, Houghton Mifflin Co., New York, 1910.

Teaching Procedures, W. C. Ruediger, Houghton Mifflin Co., New York, 1931.

Principles of Education, Ernest Norton Henderson, The MacMillan Co., 1910.

The Educative Process, William Chandler Bagley, The MacMillan Co., 1914.

School Discipline, William Chandler Bagley, The MacMillan Co., 1926.

Principles of Education, Chapman and Counts, Houghton Mifflin Co., Boston, 1924.

Elementary Principles of Education, Thorndike and Gates, The MacMillan Co., 1929.

The Philosophy of Education, H. H. Horne, The MacMillan Co., 1930.

Democratic Philosophy of Education, H. H. Horne, The MacMillan Co., 1932.

Modern Educational Theories, Boyde H. Bode, The MacMillan Co., 1927.

Meaning of Education and Other Essays, Nicholas Murray Butler, The MacMillan Co., New York, 1900.

Principles of Education, Fred Elmer Bolton, C. Scribner's Sons, New York, 1911.

Education and the Philosophy of Experimentalism, J. L. Childs, The Century Co., New York, 1931.

TEXT BOOKS IN THE HISTORY OF EDUCATION

History of Education, E. Cubberley, Houghton Mifflin Co., 1920.

Readings in The History of Education, Cubberley, Houghton Mifflin Co., 1920.

A Student's History of Education, (3 vols.) Frank Graves, The Macmillan Co., 1915.

A Text-Book in The History of Education, P. Monroe, The Macmillan Co., 1910.

Cyclopedia of Education, Paul Monroe, The MacMillan Co., 1911-12-13.

BIBLIOGRAPHY

The History of Pedagogy, Gabriel Compayré, translated with an introduction, notes, etc. by W. H. Payne, D. C. Heath & Co., Boston, 1894.

History of Education, (International Education Series), Painter, D. Appleton & Co., 1887.

Histoire Universelle de La Pédagogie, Jules Paroz, Paris, 1883.

The Evolution of The Common School, Ed. H. Reisner, The Macmillan Co., New York, 1930.

Historical Foundations of Modern Education, Ed. H. Reisner, The MacMillan Co., New York, 1927.

Nationalism and Education, Ed. H. Reisner, The MacMillan Co., 1922.

Comparative Education, I. L. Kandel, Houghton Mifflin Co., 1933.

Essays in Comparative Education, I. L. Kandel, Teachers College, Columbia University, New York, 1930.

The Reform of Secondary Education in France, I. L. Kandel, Teachers College, Columbia University, New York, 1924.

Comparative Education, Sandiford, J. M. Dent & Sons, London, E. P. Dutton Co., New York, 1918, reprinted 1927, 1929.

The New Education in Europe, F. W. Roman, George Routledge & Sons, Ltd., London, E. P. Dutton & Co., New York, 1924, revised 1929.

American Journal of Education (31 vols.), 1855-1881, edited by Henry Barnard.

HISTORY OF FRENCH LITERATURE

Causeries du Lundis (15 vols., 1851-62), **Nouveaux Lundis** (13 vols., 1863-1872), **Premiers Lundis** (3 vols. 1875), Sainte-Beuve, Paris.

Port Royal, Sainte-Beuve, (7 vols.) Librairie Hachette et Cie, 1901.

Histoire de la Littérature Française, Illustrée, Joseph Bédier et Paul Hazard, Librairie Larousse, Paris, 1923.

Manuel de l'Histoire de la Littérature Française, Fd. Brunetière, Librarie C. H. Delagrave, Paris, 1899.

Histoire de La Littérature Française, René Doumic, Librairie Classique, Paul de Laplane, Paris, 1906.

Histoire de La Littérature Française, Gustave Lanson, Librairie Hachette et Cie, Paris, 1909, (Onzième édition revue).

Histoire Illustrée de La Littérature Française, Ch. M. Des Granges, Dixième edition, Librairie Hatier, Paris, 1926.

Histoire Illustrée de La Littérature Française, Abry-Audic-Crouzet, Librairie Henri Didier, Paris, D. C. Heath & Co., Boston, 7e Edition revue el corrigée, 1912.

BOOKS OF SPECIFIC CONTENT
Rabelais

François Rabelais, Tout ce qui éxiste de ses oeuvres, Louis Moland, Garnier Frères, Libraires-éditeurs, Paris.

Rabelais, translated by Sir Thomas Urquhart, and Peter Motteux, by Harcourt, Brace & Co., New York, 1931.

French Classics For English Readers, edited by Adolphe Cohn and Curtis Page. **Rabelais,** selected and edited by Curtis Hidden Page, G. P. Putnam's Sons, New York, 1905.

The Life of Gargantua and Heroic Deeds of Pantagruel, translated by Urquhart and with an introduction by Henry Morly, Routledge & Sons, London, 1883.

Rabelais, in **Oeuvres Complètes Illustrées,** of Anatole France, Tome XVIII, Colman-Levy Éditeurs, Paris, 1927.

Rabelais, par René Millet, Librairie Hachette et Cie, Paris, 1892.

BIBLIOGRAPHY

Rabelais et Ses Oeuvres, J. Fleury, 2 vols., Paris, 1877.

Histoire Critique Des Doctrines de L'Éducation en France Depuis le Seizième Siècle, (2 vols.) Gabriel Compayré, Paris, 1883.

XVIe Siècle, Études Littéraires, Émile Faguet, Societé Française d'Imprimerie et de Librairie, Paris, 1902.

Histoire de La Littérature Française, Gustave Lanson, see above.

Histoire Illustrée de La Littérature Française, Des Granges, see above.

Rabelais, Sa Personne, Son Génie, Son Oeuvre, Paul Stapfer, Paris, 1889.

Des Idées de Rabelais et de Montaigne au Fait d'Education, in Méditations et Études Morales, Guizot, Paris, 1855.

Abelard, and The Origin and Early History of Universities, Gabriel Compayré, 1893, New York.

The Rise and Early Constitution of Universities, With a Survey of Medieval Education, S. S. Laurie (Int. Ed. Series) New York, 1887.

Educational Ideal, James Phinney Munroe, D. C. Heath & Co., Boston, 1902.

Studies in French Education From Rabelais to Rousseau, Geraldine Hodgson, Lecturer on The History and Theory of Education at University College, Bristol. Cambridge University Press, G. P. Putnam's Sons, New York, 1908.

Montaigne

Essais de Montaigne, (4 vols.), Librairie Garnier Frères, Paris.

Essayes of Montaigne, translated by John Florio and edited with an introduction and glossary by Henry Morley, University College, London, George Routledge & Sons, 1893. Also the Essays translated by Charles Cotton and revised by W. C. Hazlitt, G. Bell & Sons, London, 1926.

Montaigne, par Paul Stapfer, Librairie Hachette et Cie, Paris, 1895.

Montaigne, in XVIe Siècle, Études Littéraires, Émile, Faguet, Paris, 1902.

Des Idées de Rabelais et de Montaigne au Fait d'Education, in Méditations et Études Morales, Guizot, Paris, 1855.

L'Influence de Montaigne Sur Les Idées Pédagogiques de Locke et de Rousseau, P. Villey, Paris.

Montaigne in Histoire de La Littérature Française, G. Lanson, and also one by Des Granges, see above.

Shakespeare's Debt to Montaigne, George Coffin Tayor, Harvard University Press, Cambridge, Mass., 1925.

Studies in French Education, Hodgson, see Rabelais.

Montaigne, in History of Pedagogy, Gabriel Compayré, see above.

Educational Ideal, Munroe, see Rabelais.

Montaigne, in Representative Men, R. W. Emerson, Hurst & Co., New York.

Kindertränen, Ernst von Wildenbruch, edited by A. E. Vestling, Henry Holt & Co., New York, 1911.

Fénelon

De l'Éducation des Filles, Les Meilleurs Auteurs Classiques, Librairie Ernest Flammarion, Paris.

Dialogues sur l'éloquence, Télémaque, Dialogues des Morts, Fables, in Oeuvres Complètes, Hachette et Cie Paris.

XVIIe Siècle, Études Littéraires, Émile Faguet, Paris, see Rabelais.

Entretiens sur l'éducation des Filles, Mme de Maintenon, Paris.

Lettres sur l'Education des Filles, Mme de Maintenon, (Publiées par Th. Lavallée), Paris.

BIBLIOGRAPHY 133

Lettres Provinciales, Blaise Pascal, Paris.

Fenelon's Education of Girls, by Lupton K. Boston, 1890.

Telemachus, Adventures of, translated by Dr. Hawkesworth with a life by Lamartine, edited by O. W. Wight, Houghton Mifflin Co.

Histoire de Le Littérature Française, G. Lanson, and also the one by Des Granges, see Rabelais.

Educational Ideal, Munroe, see Rabelais.

History of Pedagogy, Compayré, see above.

Studies in French Education, Hodgson, see Rabelais.

Rousseau

Émile, ou de l'Education, Garnier Frères, Paris.

Julie ou La Nouvelle Héloise (Third Letter in the Fifth part).

Les Confessions, Le Contrat Social and Discours sur l'Origine et les Fondements de l'Inégalité, in Ouevres Complètes, Hachette et Cie, Paris, 1911.

Émile in English, Appleton Co. and also D. C. Heath Co., and a complete translation in Everyman's Library, New York.

The Social Contract, in English, George Allan and Unwin, Ruskin House, London.

A Discourse Upon the Origin and the Foundations of the Inequality Among Mankind, P. F. Collier, New York.

The Confessions of Jean-Jacques Rousseau, Gibbings and Co., London.

Rousseau, in XVIIIe Siècle, Études Littéraires, Émile Faguet, 1901, see Rabelais.

Vie et Oeuvres de J.-J. Rousseau, Avec des notes, par Albert Schinz, D. C. Heath & Co., Boston, 1921.

Rousseau and Education According to Nature, Thomas Davidson, Charles Scribners & Sons, 1930.

La Psychologie de Jean-Jacques Rousseau, Nouvelle édition, Felix Alcan, Paris, 1930.

The Early Life and Adventures of Jean-Jacques Rousseau,

Arthur Lytton Sells, W. Heffener & Sons, London, 1929.

Rousseau, 2 vols., John Morley, The MacMillan Co., New York, 1905.

Great Educators of Three Centuries, Frank Graves, The MacMillan Co., New York, 1912.

The History of Modern Elementary Education, Samuel Chester Parker, Ginn & Co., Boston, 1912.

Schools of Tomorrow, Dewey, see above.

La Herencia de Rousseau, The first chapter, by Gustavo Gili, Barcelona, Spain.

El Palacio Triste, Martinez Sierra, Ginn & Co.

The Ancient Regime, H. Taine, Henry Holt & Co. 1896.

German Education, Friedrich Paulsen, translated by T. Lorenz, T. F. Unwin, London, 1912.

Histoire de La Littérature Française, by Lanson, also the one by Des Granges, see above.

Educational Ideal, Munroe, see Rabelais.

Studies in French Education, Hodgson, see Rabelais.

Educational Reformers, R. H. Quick, Appleton Co., New

Les Précieuses Ridicules, Molières, in Oeuvres Complètes, Oxford University Press, London, 1900.

Talks to Teachers on Psychology, and To Students on Some of Life's Ideals, William James, Henry Holt & Co., New York, 1913.